Speaking
-IN-
Colors

Vernita and Nikita Nikol Naylor

B

B.E.S.T.Publishing

Speaking in Colors
Copyright ©2020 by Vernita and Nikita Nikol Naylor

ISBN 978-0-9915869-2-9 paperback
ISBN 978-0-9915869-3-6 ebook

For special discounts on bulk quantity purchases or to purchase other books from B.E.S.T. Publishing contact us at: bestpublishing@jabezenterprisegroup.com or 1-800-865-0701
http://jabezenterprisegroup.com/about-best-publishing/
100 Postmaster Drive #1718, McDonough, GA 30253
A Division of Jabez Enterprise Group (JEGroup)

Illustrations: Nikita Nikol Naylor

B.E.S.T.Publishing

SPEAKING
-IN-
COLORS

Vernita and Nikita Nikol Naylor

B.E.S.T.Publishing

Others books published by B.E.S.T. Publishing

Get the Cheese, Avoid the Traps:
An Interactive Guide to Government Contracting

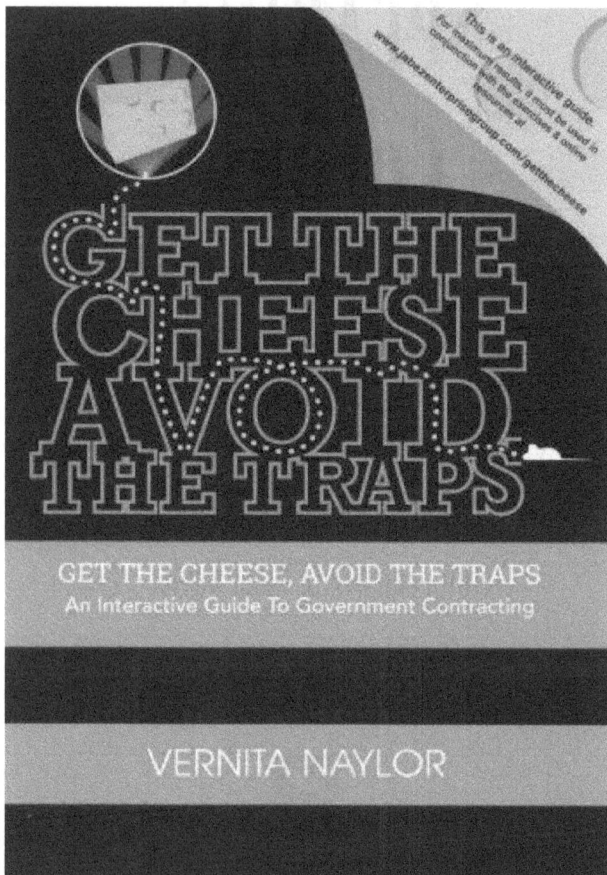

Contents

Preface i

Introduction vi

Humble Beginnings 1

Quotes 4

**First Color Frequency:
Born With 5**

Altered Carbon Copies	6
Patterns Of Frequencies	10
The World's Views	16
Born With Assessment:	
How Do You Identify?	20

**Second Color Frequency:
Nature vs. Nurture 24**

To Thyself Be True	25
Nature Vs Nurture	28
Nature Vs. Nurture Assessment:	
What Color Are You?	32

**Third Color Frequency:
Transmitting 38**

Embracing Your Color Frequency	39
Be Careful With What You Are Transmitting	43
Hurt People Hurt People	48
Toxic Filter Frequencies Are Real	54
Frequencies In Balance	61

All Abuse Is Toxic 63

All In The Family 66

Karma Is Real 71

Transmitting Assessment:
Going Deeper Within Yourself 74

Fourth Color Frequency:
Color Correction 81

Color Correction Is A Slow Process 82

Toxic Behavior Is Not Normal 87

Patience Is A Process 91

Healing Trauma And Working Towards Correction 95

Creating A Safe Place For Expressing Your Frequency 98

The Formula For Correcting Communication 102

Healthy Relationships Are Important For Healing 106

Healing Takes Time 112

Become A Leader—Others Will Follow 116

Correcting Broken Communication Patterns 119

Put On Your Mask First 121

Color Correction Assessment:
Improve Your Narrative 125

Now That We Have Your Attention 128

About the Authors 131

Vernita Naylor 131

Nikita Nikol Naylor 133

PREFACE

S*peaking in Colors* is dedicated to you, the reader, our friends, foes, family, peers, and those who have helped us through this journey of life. This book is written for you to understand what and how important "frequencies" are in helping you improve how you connect with others. What are frequencies?

Frequencies are organic energies that communicate or speak to, for, and through us. Depending on your perception (or toxic filters that we have picked up in life along the way) these frequencies can be clearly received or misunderstood. In creating this book, we have used our life experiences to create the *Speaking in Colors* concept.

This concept was created based upon the culture that we all experience and see on a daily basis and felt that something needed to be done to improve the way in which we communicate. By reading *Speaking in Colors,* you will learn about the four frequencies and how they are crucial for effective communication. These four frequencies are the essential elements in communicating because they allow you to become familiar with and aware of your communication style and that of others.

Additionally, you will learn how frequencies can greatly impact and create effective communication to reach your desired goal or become inefficient, causing you to lose time, money, and the inability to accomplish your purpose. How you communicate is important because at any given time in today's society you will find at least four (4) generations within the same space. Within this space you can meet anyone from the Silent Generation, Baby Boomers and Millennial to Gen Z each experiencing their own biases and 'Isms' (ageism, racism, sexism, classism, and ableism).

Communication will always play a vital role in how your relationships are built, maintained, and under-stood. By learning about your color frequency and the ways in which you transmit your frequency will be instrumental to your success.

As you begin to embrace the *Speaking in Colors* concept, you will discover that, within each frequency phase you learn something new and different about yourself and others around you. Much like seeing the same movie or reading the same book each occurrence creates a different outcome and perspective if you're open to it. As you continue to embrace the same fre-quencies you will obtain the same experiences but as new frequencies are being introduced so are your new experiences.

Communication is Power. It is tremendously useful and effective when there is a safe space being created that allows others to freely express themselves. It is more necessary to create this safe space when you encounter those you believe are different from you.

During these times, regardless of the situation or circumstance you may find yourself in, it is a must to begin to work on fully understanding how to transition into effective communication with those you perceive are different or may operate in a unique fashion. Also, it is important to bridge the gap allowing for an environment of learning and proper usage of these color frequencies to establish effective communication.

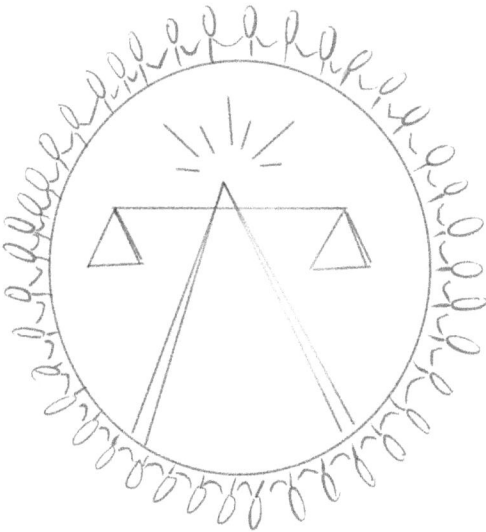

HANDS around the WORLD

You will discover by reading this book that the *Speaking in Colors* concept presents how color frequencies represent our individual behavior, character, and personality traits. Similar to astrology, and other personality tests, nothing is absolute, but these evaluations provide us with a guide into who we are. Our color frequencies also represent our diversity which includes our uniqueness, out-of-the-box thinking, and creativity that contributes major value.

How we communicate with others resonates with the results we have obtained using these principles. This book offers the tools necessary to be able to convey the message you intend and communicate it clearly. These tools can be taught and put in practice in any platform or setting (diversity studies, management, leadership, personal development, business development, entrepreneurship and sensitivity training). The information is so simple and easy to learn that you can teach it on all levels from formative schooling (K12-University) and the workplace to community settings.

We believe that there are four transitions of frequencies. These four frequencies can impact your communication outcomes:

~: THE FREQUENCY you were BORN WITH

~: THE FREQUENCY given by NATURE VS. NURTURE

~: TRANSMITTING FREQUENCY

~: COLOR CORRECTION FREQUENCY

JOIN US on this exciting journey to learn how you too can be effective in *Speaking in Colors*. If you are ready to receive it, this book will change your life! By reading and embracing the concepts of *Speaking in Colors*, you will be able to:

~: Take the stress out of communicating, while building self-confidence

~: Effectively communicate in all forms of circumstances and situations; and

~: Learn how to work with those who are different from you or who seem difficult to work with

Speaking in Colors is not only a concept, it's A MOVEMENT!

JOIN THE MOVEMENT

Welcome to the Speaking in Colors Community. We want to hear from you. Connect with us!
https://jabezenterprisegroup.com/speakingincolors/

INTRODUCTION

N o matter where in the world you live, in many ways we are the same. Our primary goals or concerns stem from our need to communicate one to another. If you look closely you will discover that, within our need to communicate, we express a wide range of frequencies from love, fear, and happiness, to anger, all with the common goal to convey and express our feelings and desires through making a connection.

When we veer too far off into the path of toxic expression and unclear communication we become distracted and convoluted in our own frequencies. When the toxicity has reached its peak there is a natural grounding that needs to take place. Through this grounding balance is restored and we are realigned back to our initial goals and intent.

At times this happens on a personal level but can also happen on a regional, national or global level, depending on the severity of the imbalance. Look at how a crisis like 9/11 brought people together from all races, genders, creed and social status. A crisis such as that created a commonality that allowed us to bypass our differences and focus on our initial reason for being.

During times like these, people are willing to come together for an alliance of common good or purpose to restore balance. You also see this happening in other situations and circumstances around the world, in the form of groups raising awareness regarding pollution, protests for a violation of civil rights, petitions to influence and change laws or finding a cure for a devastating disease to save lives. At some point no matter your social or economic status we will all be affected and impacted by some of these same types of occurrences.

We are all connected through six degrees of separation, and this circle is becoming even smaller. According to the *Science Alert* article "Are We Really All Connected By Just Six Degrees of Separation? by Fiona MacDonald, (August 27, 2015), those six degrees are being reduced due to people becoming connected through social media. If nothing else, take comfort in the fact that no matter how lonely you feel, one of your acquaintances could be the key to putting you in touch with someone who will change your life in just six (or less) steps."

What does all this mean to you? You must be ready and fully equipped to effectively balance yourself and communicate your needs. At times it can be our differences that create the inability to communicate, or a lack of fully understanding all aspects of how to communicate.

Speaking in Colors will educate you on the concept of who, what, when, where, why, and how effective communication or ineffective communication can occur. Balance is the key. Knowing how to balance these communication frequencies is necessary for your success.

Humble Beginnings

Growing up in West Oakland, California, was both good and bad, much like most diverse urban communities in the world. Regardless of what was happening in or around our community my parents did their best to help guide us along the path of gaining the best of all things: education, career and life, while stressing to us the importance of living to our fullest potentials.

I would enjoy watching my father create and develop so many things for us to enjoy within and around our home. His entrepreneurial spirit was something I was proud of the most. I watched how he navigated to get things done, which helped me understand how the frequencies around us can shape, impact, and influence our lives. I also realized that there were several frequency variations - both high and low- that were continually interacting and connecting with us.

Once I began to better understand the essential aspects of these frequences, I was able to make conscious decisions as whether to embrace and connect with these frequencies or learn not to react to them at all. These decisions were extremely important once I found myself working and thriving within a variety of industries where it was crucial to be mindful of how I spoke, reacted and the languages I used with those I was tasked to work with.

Depending on what environment I found myself working in, I needed to listen, learn, hear, and understand what made the people tick and show them that I could relate to their needs as they transitioned into the different aspects of their lives. I learned to be inclusive and understanding of various frequencies (youth, adults, business and music industry professionals, White House officials and alike) which helped me to communicate more effectively, be heard and understood with true intent.

When speaking to an audience of any size it is important to CONNECT, this can be challenging. When connecting it is critical to be flexible and adjust accordingly to varying behaviors, personalities, and character traits of your audience, while not allowing any low frequencies from others to impact your intended results. It was through these experiences that I began to develop the *Speaking in Colors* concept. I discovered that I was able to communicate with these frequencies and found a way to understand the impact I carried in the outcome with different frequencies.

In turn, I then taught not only my daughter—who has been able to successfully improve the concept—but that of others within our tight-knit community of family and friends.

Speaking in Colors is not only a movement but a way of exchanging ideas, information, and intelligence. It is a movement to create a paradigm shift in how we think, express, transmit, and view each other.

QUOTES

"....we're all members of the same race. The human race."
~Jane Elliott

"If you meet someone's frequency that is not aligned with yours, send them love and move along."
~Dr. Wayne Dyer

"Full diversity and inclusion would only happen if we stop 'acting' to fit in. It starts with ourselves. We need to have the courage to share our perspectives while being mindful how to convey it at the table and be proud of our uniqueness without fear of backlash."
~Lih Fang Chew

"The only source of knowledge is experience."
~Albert Einstein

"Diversity is a necessity born out of adversity to rebalance a portfolio, to revive a company and to reunite a nation. If Diversity was a deliverable, then Inclusion drives it."
~Johnson Hor

"It is time for parents to teach young people early on that in diversity there is beauty and there is strength."

~Maya Angelou

First Color Frequency:
Born With

Altered Carbon Copies

O ur mind and perception dictate the way in which we communicate. The essence of who we are, how we operate, and what creates our behavior patterns and perception were formed by our life experiences. Although similar we are vastly different. If we were all alike we would not be able to enjoy the variety of things we do today. We would not be able to communicate and reflect a continuation of change and a connection between a sender and a receiver. With every aspect of communication, even as polar opposites, we have yet varying similarities of understanding, which make things interesting.

In order to really understand how to communicate effectively, we need to change how we think and look at

things. The main way we communicate is through frequencies. Everything around us communicates this way, from sea life and insects to plants.

EXAMPLE

Watch when the trees sway as they connect with the wind and the leaves fall as they connect with the Earth, or see the bees connect as they kiss the flowers they pollinate.

Remember, frequencies are organic energies that communicate or speak to, for, and through us. The main purpose of frequencies are to communicate a message. Frequency exchanges are occurring all around you, and if you stop and watch closely, you will see that there are times when communication has occurred but the connection has been lost. You may not always be aware that you have given off an unintended frequency until you notice that you are not obtaining your desired results when communicating.

Become a people watcher and watch as people come together in a room for a party or a conference. There are some who may appear awkward in this type of setting and may never make a connection, while there are others who move about and connect fluidly. In these examples, the essence of frequencies are at the root of all things, in whether a connection is made or not.

As people try to connect, what makes the difference is how the frequencies were sent and received by each party. In this form of communication the messages being conveyed between all parties involved is what makes the difference.

EXAMPLE

A sequence of words can be conveyed in a message, or written content can be read, but the end result can be received differently, causing contrasting results and outcomes.

This occurs because frequencies emit and receive an exchange of information, intelligence, or ideas uniquely. Due to us all being different and living various lives, it is important to know and understand that we are each programmed in our own individual unique fashion. The only way to understand another's viewpoint is to be willing to connect with their frequency.

How you do this is by accepting and reprogramming your mind. This paradigm shift gives you the ability to effectively communicate with those around you. Clear communication is essential and can be crucial in how it impacts our lives.

When attempting to connect the frequencies that you communicate with can build up or tear down, motivate or demoralize. In order to become an effective communicator and to obtain the results we desire, it is important to be accepting and to create a space for others to express themselves freely without judgment.

An important question to ask yourself is how effective are you at communicating? This is where and how frequencies are being channeled. These channels of frequencies have numerous forms of energy when being transmitted. As previously stated you will notice that at any given time most often, there are at least four generations in one space.

Within that one space various races, cultures, and religions are around you, all interacting, which widens the range of communications and frequencies in that space. These frequencies are not only tied to generations, races, cultures, or religions, they are also tied to *Colors* which represents our behavior, character, and personality traits.

These traits which are tied to *Colors* represent how we communicate and connect. When we communicate, our color frequency represents our diversity, which determines the outcome of our connection. Our diversity contributes and brings value to the table, especially in an environment in which everyone can be heard and feel safe to express their opinions. This diversity can be a win-win for everyone if the diversity of others—the differences—are accepted.

EXAMPLE

If a millennial inventor wants to discuss a product idea with a baby boomer investor, the frequencies being emitted between the two are important because, despite the differences, there must be a connection in order for the investment to be made. For this to happen an understanding must occur. As the understanding transpires then a connection happens and the idea is sold.

To sell the idea, the millennial must focus not only on understanding his own frequency, but also that of the baby boomer. The baby boomer must do the same in order to understand what the millennial is attempting to convey. Through this connection the inventor convinces the investor to provide the funding necessary for the product.

This interaction can be a win-win for not only each individual participating in this transaction but the world, this is how new products are being introduced into the marketplace. Verbal communication is one of the leading frequencies that human beings use to interact with each other. But it is also one of the leading frequencies of misunderstanding. Written communication comes in second in being a misunderstood form of communication because both are affected by the sender's and receiver's communication style and perception.

Patterns of Frequencies

Verbal frequencies transmit and exchange information, and intelligence and emits different types of communication responses between individuals and groups, primarily because of how the frequencies are being sent and received. According to *Webster's Dictionary*, communication reflects words, sounds, signs or actions that exchange or express a thought, idea, or feeling. *Wikipedia* describe communication as verbal, non-verbal, written or oral communication between beings. Frequencies are all around us and communicate continually.

EXAMPLE

Have you ever found yourself saying that a piece of fashion, furniture, or vehicle is speaking to you, and your internal voice says, I must buy it? Or what about after a rough day when you can't wait to go to the beach or sit at the park to unwind and calm your spirit? Do any of these examples resonate with you? These are frequencies connecting with you either through a tangible or an intangible frequency field.

As a human being we most often are gifted with an unique vocal frequency. For some the vocal frequency can be deep, raspy, soft, or loud and expressive. Our voice is the initial tool given to us by the universe to allow us the ability to communicate our frequencies verbally.

Our vocal frequencies, mixed with intent and words, convey a message to the receiver. Although we are given these tools of communication in our infancy, we are not initially aware of how to use them. Beginning in infancy, we are BORN WITH frequencies that expresses who we really are, which begins to develop and teach us a strong sense of self.

It is during early childhood, that we are left to practice, learn, and become familiar with our own frequencies by the stimulation of energy around us through our five senses. In our childhood we are more sensitive to the connection of frequencies that surround us. These connections are the feelings that begin to resonate through our five senses, introducing us to the world and a wide range of color frequencies offered to us within the universe.

These senses transmit frequency exchange through taste, sight, sound, smell, and touch. When you touch and feel the warmth of your parents, or sit in your favorite chair, frequencies are being stimulated. Frequencies can also be embraced through the smell, taste, and flavors of foods, bringing you back to your culture, childhood, or a special place.

Color frequencies begin to connect with us beginning in our formative years. These color frequencies help to formulate our behavior, character, and personality traits. As children, we begin to learn about the world and in how it communicates through the frequency of colors. Boys are encouraged to wear blue, while little girls are encouraged to wear pink. As adults, men will wear a lot of browns, dark or muted colors, while women are encouraged to like bright colors and be drawn to hues of red.

Watch a child at play and you will begin to see how important color frequencies are in our lives. A child's life is filled with the ebbs and flow of emotions, and during these times, colors reflect their moods. Children learn to connect colors in their effort to communicate and express themselves to the outside world.

EXAMPLE

When children play with their favorite toy, most experience the sights and sounds the toy transmits through color frequencies. When they are happy, they may pick up something yellow to maintain that feeling, while if they are feeling sad or depressed, blue or black objects seem to attract them.

How Do Bright Colors Appeal to Kids? by Rachel Pancare (Sciencing, updated April 23, 2018): "Children take in the world around them through their eyes, and bright colors are one of the first aspects of sight that help them distinguish form and categorize objects. These colors appeal to young children, as they are easier for them to see. At about 5 months old, children can see colors with their still-developing vision, though distinguishing bright colors comes easier to them. As children age, they continue to be drawn to brighter colors. Color has also been known to affect their moods and behavior."

As children begin to develop and grow, they master their frequency by being drawn to colors that closely associate them with how they wish to express themselves. The irony is, as children we did not know it, but we were actually *Speaking in Colors*. As we grow we often allow misconceptions to occur about people based on how they look as well as the color of the clothes they wear.

What are your thoughts when you see a person wearing certain colors? Do you actually believe that the color of the clothes people wear reflects their story? People who wear black are considered dark, stern, mysterious, and misunderstood, while it is perceived that those wearing bright colors are upbeat, optimistic, energetic, and popular. But what about those who wear colors like green, purple, or any of the other "neutral" colors?

Color frequencies play a major part in how we interact with society and the world around us.

EXAMPLE

In school when our teachers grade our papers for good work, we may receive a blue or green mark, or gold star. If our paper needs improvement, comments are most often written in red or urgent colors accompanied with an unwelcomed grade. Even before we thoroughly review the paper or see the comments written on it, we prejudge what we think is being said about the paper based on the colors of the comments.

What about when we see a red mark on a utility or credit card bill? Even before we read the expected "Past Due," we have already developed a reaction to what we believe it will say. All of these examples are signs of how colors affect our world.

The World's Views

As we go deeper into the BORN WITH frequency principle it is important to understand that communication challenges occur when we do not understand how to connect with others due to our own internal biases (also known as "Isms",) and issues. Our internal biases are obtained and influenced by other frequencies around us, such as the media (social, print or broadcast), our own life experiences and interactions with those that are the closest to us. These initial biases are normally established upon first impressions of what we hear, see, and feel.

As we grow older, this philosophy sometimes changes as we begin to judge people based upon other factors and first impressions. Through our history and experiences, we are often taught to prejudge a person's story based upon the color of their skin, we often learn that people are not who we perceive them to be. People never truly understand the various layers of whom we really are—unless they ask.

We must be conscious enough to understand that prejudging is not the correct way to categorize others. We know it is wrong, but we still do it. Understanding these layers reflects that we are not the "skin" that we are in.

John Friedrich Blumenbach was a German physician, naturalist, physiologist and anthropologist in the 1700s divided the human species into five races:

- ~: Red–North American Natives
- ~: Brown–Hispanics, Pacific Islanders
- ~: Black–Sub-Saharan Africans
- ~: Yellow–East Asians
- ~: White–Caucasians, Europeans

Source: Wikipedia, Historical Race Concepts, March 10, 2020, and John Friedrich Blumenbach, Racial Anthropology, March 25, 2020.

How do you identify within these five categories? Do you fit into only one category or do several of them speak to you? These differing hues of the skin began the essence of communication.

Early in man's development, groups or tribes of people who looked alike according to their skin color were able to identify and effectively communicate with each other. Later, there were some groups who begin to experience a breakdown in communication, causing years of fighting and destruction. But others were able to continue to connect and interact in a very cohesive manner, resulting in survival and progression.

As life evolved, experiences forced groups of humans to interact, communicate, and connect with those who were different from themselves, just as other species of mammals have done for survival.

EXAMPLE

The BBC nature documentary "Blue Planet II" showed what happened when bottlenose dolphins were being hunted by false killer whales. Once approached, the bottlenose dolphins' changed their frequencies and began to communicate and connect with the predatory whales. This connection caused the attack to cease and instead created a united front between the bottlenose dolphins and the false killer whales to attack other sea life for survival; the enemy became an ally through frequencies.

Throughout the centuries, shifts in methods of survival became necessary due to migration and transition. Such adaptation allowed tribes and groups of people to go to the next level. People began to see and understand that we are all divinely connected, regardless of the color of our skin. It is also understood that, in most cases, our skin color does provide the nucleus of who we are and what we represent.

Communication can be used to either help or hurt because of the frequencies in which the messages are being conveyed or received. When you communicate, begin to look at the frequencies which you resonate. Do the frequencies convey who you really are and what you are trying to say to the world or is a different message being conveyed?

Despite its challenges, communication can be robust and exhilarating. Each person in the universe has a different story to tell. No two birth communication frequencies are exactly alike, not even with identical twins.

Understanding the color frequency you are BORN WITH, will help you understand yourself and those around you. The next time you encounter someone different; *challenge yourself* by giving them a chance. Do not prejudge them. No matter where you meet. Learn their story.

Understand that it is important that you first know about and learn your own frequency in order to better understand the frequency of others. During the BORN WITH Assessment you will learn the steps necessary to create a space of comfort while learning more about who you are.

BORN WITH ASSESSMENT: HOW DO YOU IDENTIFY?

Take some time and think about how society sees you. Were you called inappropriate names throughout your life? Understanding who you are and how you identify is important, not what others think or believe about you. In this assessment, the focus will be on changing the narrative of how you view others based upon the undertones and the hues of their skin. It is important to understand that our skin does not tell the whole story of who we are. To fully understand the BORN WITH frequency, make sure that you complete all three (3) exercises.

Step 1. John Friedrich Blumenbach, a German physician, naturalist, physiologist and anthropologist in the 1700s, divided the human species into five races: red, brown, black, yellow, and white.
Source: Wikipedia, Historical Race Concepts, March 10, 2020, and John Friedrich Blumenbach, Racial Anthropology, March 25, 2020.

Below, circle which **one** color you believe most closely **resembles you when someone initially looks at you.** Remember that most of us have more than one lineage within our blood line pertaining to our ancestry. Even if you are considered multi-cultured, **choose only one color:**

- ଋ: Red–North American Natives
- ଋ: Brown–Hispanics, Pacific Islanders
- ଋ: Black–Sub-Saharan Africans
- ଋ: Yellow–East Asians
- ଋ: White–Caucasians, Europeans

Based on the one category that you chose, what do you believe others think about you when they 'initially' see you? Have you heard others say things about you that aren't true? Can you see the prejudice of others you encounter, or do they seem more accepting?

Are others interested in knowing more about you? How do others make you feel? Now consider do you judge others using the same parameters?

It is human nature for people to inflict upon you the story they are familiar with, not your truth. Each time you are in a conversation and someone makes the mistake of dictating your story, change the narrative by helping them to see you in a different light. Without your help, people will continue to tell the story about you or others like you based on the skin color they see.

If you change your self-talk about how you see others, then maybe, others will begin to change theirs about how they see you and others.

Step 2. Start journaling by writing down a few points of some things that people may be shocked to know about you. As you begin to communicate with others, try to break the ice by sharing some of these shocking facts and see how they respond. This process helps to improve the frequency of what we are BORN WITH. The objective is to assure that, regardless of how different others are or seem to you, create a space of freedom and safety.

The type of environment you create will allow others to feel inclusive with the ability to speak freely, because they will feel that their voices and input are being heard and considered. The safer others feel in expressing themselves, the more constructive the conversation becomes. The more constructive the conversation becomes, the better the results.

Step 3. The next time that you are in a group setting try these quick and easy steps to create a place of safety and acceptance:

- ∾: Smile, make eye contact, or say hello
- ∾: Incite small talk to create a comfortable space
- ∾: Invite them to tell their own story in whatever form they choose
- ∾: Actively listen to and hear what they have to say
- ∾: Analyze what they say and see how it aligns with what you thought of them.

As you navigate through these three exercises, what are your thoughts? What did you learn about yourself? What did you discover about your interaction with others? Did you learn something new? Did you find yourself embracing others and learning that they're not the skin that they're in? Or did you continue to judge them despite hearing or learning something different about them?

> *Let's stop believing that our differences make*
> *us superior or inferior to one another ...*
> *Let's not be afraid that our different colors*
> *make us different people ...*

> ~Miguel Angel Ruiz

SECOND COLOR FREQUENCY: NATURE VS. NURTURE

To Thyself Be True

Frequencies are trying to speak, communicate, and connect all around us. Everything emits frequencies.

EXAMPLE

When seeing or smelling a field of lavender flowers, for some people it creates an aura of calm and peace, while for others it does nothing. It is the same when sitting by the ocean for some it motivates and stimulates, but for others there is no response or reaction.

One day sit and watch children at play, how they innately choose a leader and instinctively in most cases the other children follow. Your nature and how you were nurtured play an important part in who you are today. These factors will determine how your communication skills are developed and whether or not you can connect with others.

Our nature reflects our innate abilities in how we react and respond to situations and circumstances. These reactions will help you understand when faced with tough decisions, whether you are a fighter, a survivor, or do you tend to quickly succumb to the environment or circumstance you encounter? It is important that we know who we are and what stimulates us. We all have different motivating factors that influence us.

For some we are influenced by our upbringing, while for others they are led by what they've been told or what they see in the media and their surrounding environment. The ultimate goal is to be true to who you are. Once you are comfortable with yourself, you can then learn to become comfortable with others. In most cases it is those who feel insecure about themselves, that tend to have a problem and will quickly reject others.

> *Authenticity is about being true to who you are, even when everyone around you wants you to be someone else.*
>
> ~Michael Jordan

People are attracted to authenticity. People are in awe with those who are confident. Being genuine stimulates leadership abilities.

Some lead while others follow. In achieving excellence, authenticity is crucial, especially in a leader. You may not consider yourself a leader, but others might.

When you discover that you can positively influence others, and notice that their interactions with you influence them for the better, you are a leader of truth. You are being true to who you are, and people are embracing it through their interaction and connection with you. They are becoming one with your frequency.

WHO RU?

As our nature continues to evolve, how we were nurtured—our upbringing or the things that influenced us during our formative years—begin to take form as well. This is how the second frequency NATURE VS. NURTURE evolves and shapes our original frequency. The various layers of our natural nature verses how we were nurtured impact us tremendously. In our formative years we connect with our natural frequencies as we learn how to express our creativity through drawings, the color we select to illustrate with or the color of the toys that we are drawn to.

We also see examples of this during our teenage years when selecting clothing, shoes, hair color, or hairstyle; these choices reflect the beginning of us expressing our natural frequencies and creating our identity. Our outer appearance is one thing, but what we are experiencing internally emits frequencies as well.

Transitioning from childhood with feelings of

abandonment, diversity biases, or "Isms"—ableism (dis-
ability), racism, ageism, classism, sexism—isolation,
feeling alone, separate or shut out, happiness, peer pressure, body image, love and making life decisions begins
to take root. These essential elements formulate who
we feel we are to become. During the teenage years,
people tend to get stuck and allow others to define
them, causing them to rebel or engage, depending upon
how they are taught to deal with life challenges.

The goal is to not allow low frequencies to change or
dilute your natural frequency levels, regardless of the
influence or circumstance. As we take everything from
our childhood and teenage years into our adulthood,
we create yet another type of frequency. As adults we
become more definitive about who we are, where we are
going and where we are willing to draw the line. At each
phase of our lives, there is a continuous ebb and flow,
were we speak and communicate through transmitting
and embracing frequencies.

Nature vs Nurture

Now that you understand that everything around
us emit frequencies, let's see how it affects us in other
ways. The frequency being conveyed to us, either
through nature or nurture speaks through an organic
flow. NATURE VS. NURTURE is an important element
because it will show up in your frequency makeup,

reflecting whether or not you can make a solid connection. We each have a different frequency when dealing with nature and nurturing; even as identical twins.

Although twins can be identical, in many ways their response to events, situations, or circumstances can be very different. How we each communicate or speak through our frequencies depends upon various sources. Mother Nature plays a part in the frequency interaction as well. Looking at the beautiful yellow and orange leaves falling from the trees not only signals that autumn is coming but may incite within you some beautiful memories of the past.

At the aquarium you are made aware that the blue-ringed octopus is dangerous, harmful and venomous but you are drawn to its frequency of bright, vibrant colors any way. Listen to and hear the sounds of the birds chirping at the crack of dawn. Feel the bliss and relax as you see aqua-colored waves crash against the shore.

There is nothing we must do to receive this type of communication; it just happens naturally, organically. This is also true in the form of nurturing and the frequencies that we attain. As we evolve through life, we begin to see and understand how colors organically influence our lives. As we get older, we start to make the connection with our personal frequencies as they relate to the world around us.

Within each of us there is a frequency that is attached to a color. With each color, a behavior, personality and character trait is associated with it. As we grow older, our color frequencies and that of others begin to mean more in our lives, especially as we begin to communicate more often without getting the results we desire. It is important to be mindful as to how we are connecting.

Have you noticed what happens when you are talking to others? How do you appear and come across to them when you are communicating? Are you condescending, passive-aggressive, kind, or _____? Do people appear irritated, emotional, or unresponsive when talking to you? If you notice that you continually do not get the results you desire, begin to reflect on why? Ask yourself, how long has this been happening?

Could it be something in your past, like how you were nurtured, or simply your nature that is causing this rift? Reflect on what type of nurturing you received growing up. Were you raised in a shouting home or surrounded by people who were non-expressive? This could be a part of your nurturing frequency which is influencing your nature.

What about guardians or foster parents who raised you? Did they continually reflect on oppressive sexist, class, or racist behaviors that made you look skeptically at others? Everything that surrounds us, especially during our formative and teenage years, impacts and greatly affects how we interact as adults. You may not realize it, but if you were to take a closer look at how you were nurtured, you will discover some similarities of who you have become or are becoming is because of your upbringing.

Sometimes, you will also discover that, despite some differences, your behavior, personality, and character emit frequencies that has been passed on from generation to generation. As everyone expresses themselves and is connected through nature or nurture frequencies, the outcome or the results occurring will be determined. How your nature or how you were nurtured will reflect your response when reacting to lower level frequencies versus positive level frequencies. These reactions can range from feeling unaccepted and threatened to included and heard.

As you become one with Mother Nature, listen with intent. For effective communication, focus on how your frequency is organically being tapped into, and learn what is being said to you. When you encounter someone or something different from you, like with Mother Nature, don't prejudge, but stop and listen for the messages being shared with you.

NATURE VS NURTURE

NATURE VS. NURTURE
ASSESSMENT:
WHAT COLOR ARE YOU?

For the sake of getting you started in improving your communication frequency, let's take an assessment test to gauge where you are right now. Every color of the rainbow represents a behavior, character, or personality trait. These traits are called your color frequency. These color frequencies represent your diversity which reflects your uniqueness, and what you bring to the table.

It is through your diversity where your color frequency influences the exchange of ideas, information, and intelligence, in an open and out-of-the-box fashion. Most personalities fall within the primary color chart but on some occasions the reader may obtain a result within the secondary color chart as well. Primary Colors: Red, Blue and Yellow and Secondary Colors: Purple, Green and Orange. Those who fall into the Secondary Color frequency are those that have more than one Primary Color frequency for their behavior, character or personality trait depending upon the situation or circumstance.

Choose fifteen words from the following list that best/most describe you in any type of situation or circumstance. Words mean different things to different people; feel empowered to research any words that you are unclear as to their true definition and meaning:

Spontaneous		Aggressive	
Proficient		Optimistic	
Generous		Expert	
Thoughtful		Compassionate	
Warm		Social	
Irrational		Unfriendly	
Suppressive		Loyal	
Exhibitionist		Motivated	
Impulsive		Tranquil	
Uncertain		Insincere	
Brilliant		Dislike Change	
Vigorous		Nervous	
Sincere		Envious	
Cheap		Cheerful	
Jealous		Active	
Quiet		Superficial	
Extrovert		Flamboyant	
Anxious		Peaceful	
Rigid			
Lives For the Moment			

Review the overview of what each color frequency represent:

ORANGE (Social Communicator)

You are comfortable being around people and can operate in any type of social setting.
HIGH: Extrovert, Warm, Flamboyant, Optimistic
LOW: Insincere, Exhibitionist, Superficial, Cheap

RED (Empowered)

You exude confidence and have a high self-esteem.
HIGH: Active, Cheerful, Optimistic
LOW: Impulsive, Vigorous, Aggressive

YELLOW (Mindfulness)

You are free spirited and thoughtful of others.
HIGH: Live for the Moment, Motivated, Spontaneous, Social
LOW: Anxious, Nervous, Uncertain

PURPLE (Creative)

You use an artistic approach and method.
HIGH: Peaceful, Quiet, Tranquil, Compassionate, Generous
LOW: Irrational, Suppressive

BLUE (Acceptance)

You are accommodating and inclusive of others.
HIGH: Loyal, Sincere, Thoughtful
LOW: Rigid, Dislike Change, Unfriendly

GREEN (Practical)

You deal with things in a basic manner.
HIGH: Brilliant, Proficient, Expert
LOW: Envious, Jealous

Next to each of the fifteen words you have chosen, place the letter from the list that relates to the color frequency trait. For example, if one of your words from the list is "Loyal," place the letter B next to it; "Nervous" is a Y, "Optimistic" is O and R (which has two color personality traits, put both letters next to it on your paper), and so on. Then count the number of times each frequency letter appears in your list. **The color with the highest number is your color frequency.**

This is how to arrive at your results. If you have 2 Bs, 4 Ys, 3 Os, and 6 Rs, then based upon these results, you are closely associated with the color frequency RED. Red=Empowered because you had 6 Rs.

Your *Speaking in Colors* assessment test results closely reflect who you are and what your color frequency represents according to your communication style. Your assessment results could reflect more than two color frequencies. If this is the case with your results, it can mean that you communicate differently depending upon the situation or circumstance.

EXAMPLE

While my daughter has only one color frequency, Purple, which fits her creative frequency but for myself I have two frequencies: Red=Empowered and Y=Mindfulness. For me this means that when I am in work mode, I operate in Red (Empowered), but in my personal life I operate in Yellow (Mindfulness).

Much like other personality tests and astrology, all is not absolute, but they do provide you with a guide to understanding yourself and how you speak and communicate. A breakdown in communication usually occurs due to the different approaches to life and in how the message is being conveyed and understood. Understanding your color frequency is the goal, stay focused on these results as you navigate through the rest of the book.

As you begin to embrace who you are, and learn to love and accept yourself the frequency you emit will instill love and acceptance towards others. Learning how to embrace and accept others in who they are and in how they communicate will allow you the ability to tailor your own frequency in making a positive connection. This process is one of the many ways to help improve your color frequency and in connecting with others.

It is important to remember that you cannot change others, but you can change your response to them when communicating. By creating a positive connection, you will be able to accomplish the goals and obtain the deliverables that you desire. Embrace your color frequency and learn what works best in how to communicate. Take your time and enjoy the process!

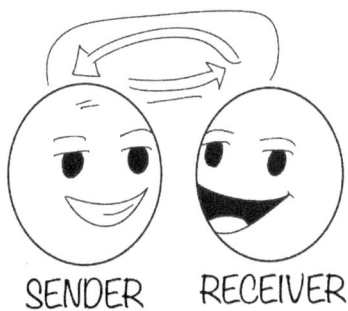

SENDER   RECEIVER

Third Color Frequency: Transmitting

Embracing Your Color Frequency

The results of your color frequency assessment test represent who you are and where the third frequency TRANSMITTING speaks. Just like astrology, or other personality tests, there may be some behavior, character, or personality variations within you that cause you the ability to be unable to connect with someone else. On several occasions you will notice there are some glaring similarities as well regardless of our nature or how we were nurtured during frequency transmission.

When communicating we subconsciously create and stimulate each other in a particular way, especially when interacting with those we feel comfortable with. When we feel uncomfortable, we tend to find ways to subconsciously not connect by initially judging, avoiding, intimidating, or becoming non-responsive.

Colors influence our lives in several ways. Warm colors—reds, yellows, and oranges— represent coziness and security that many people use for their fireplaces, kitchens, or washrooms, while cool colors—greens, blues, and violets—are considered refreshing, inviting, and calming. It is important that we try to connect with people in the same way that these colors do.

Every aspect of our lives helps to organically create and transmit frequencies. When you acknowledge and communicate with others, you are generating a connection through transmitted energy represented by colors. The main question is, is the connection you are emitting reflecting a high or a low color frequency? Are you garnering the results that you are seeking?

Once you begin to embrace your color frequency it is important to understand how to connect. As the sender, when communicating, you can gauge whether the desired results of your color frequency were properly received, based upon the response in connection to the receiver.

EXAMPLE

If you are a Social Communicator (Orange) make sure that you are emitting a warm, optimistic frequency, rather than being superficial and insincere.

It is when we start to create a safe place in this world by the frequencies we are sending or receiving that we begin the journey to growth. Growth only occurs when acceptance has been embraced. Remember that everyone is not vibrationally at the same place and may not desire to become accepting and acquire growth.

At some point as an adult, you have to be able to

master how to express the message you want to convey via voice or body language when you are communicating. In order to become effective in communicating, you must process how your color frequencies are being received. Watch your body language. It is not always what you say but what your body is TRANSMITTING as well that makes the difference.

There are several steps to determine how we transmit our frequencies. Below are some simple steps to consider to begin the path of successfully communicating and connecting:

~: First, you must learn about the different variations of color frequencies. This is like learning and overstanding different types of people, especially those we feel indifferent about.

~: Second, as you can see from your assessment test results, there are different types of behavior, character, and personality traits—from social communicator, and empowered to creative—associated with colors. Each of these traits are connected to colors which display why some traits connect easily while others do not.

~: Third, as you look more closely at those you are attempting to connect with, do you know what their color frequency is? In most cases, no, but the ultimate goal is to find some way to make a connection.

∻: Last, begin to look at all of these factors, as you embrace your color frequency and tap into the persons, groups, or audience you are attempting to connect with. Learn how to accept others as they are and embrace their differences while focusing on what you have in common, which is needed to reach your desired goals.

As you walk through each step, understand that this is a process and you will not change overnight. Any type of process takes a while to cultivate because you are not only dealing with changing a pattern that is a part of your nature or in how you were nurtured, but you are now learning how to incorporate something new and different into your life. You were created through several stages and phases, beginning with the various situations and circumstances you have encountered in your upbringing, past, environment, and in this world.

In order to gain the best form of communication, the goal is to always stay within the positive spectrum when you speak. Staying within the positive spectrum is to remain among the higher vibrational color frequency as we explored with the Social Communicator (Orange) example. It is always important to be mindful of how you are TRANSMITTING information. Continue to focus on being a better person, loving, accepting and non-judgmental. Be true to who you are, and get better at doing it.

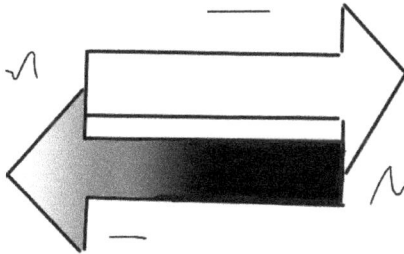

Be Careful With What You Are Transmitting

All of life is energy and we are transmitting it at every moment.

~Oprah Winfrey

There are several things that are being transmitted to us on a daily basis. When we transmit information through communication, it is important to always remain within the positive spectrum of your color frequency in order to connect effectively. What this means is that when you wake up to start your day perform an attitude assessment. An attitude assessment is to simply check to see what type of mood that you are experiencing.

If you notice that you are already experiencing feelings of sadness, depression or any other type of low feelings find out why? Understand that you can quickly be persuaded to respond and interact with others through low frequencies if you do not check in with yourself to find out why. By remaining within this spectrum of negativity it is likely that you will encounter others that are negative, unpleasant and not in alignment with your color frequency that can greatly impact your day.

Webster states that to "transmit" is to send, convey, cause, hand down, forward, or spread something from a person or place to another. Watch how you start your day. See what occurs when you begin to transmit energy through your color frequency, especially when you encounter those you do not agree with due to their appearance, the color of their skin, culture, religion, or how they communicate.

When you are TRANSMITTING information, your frequency is emitting energy that either makes a connection or causes a rejection.

EXAMPLE

You may come into someone's office or personal space and, after a time, begin to feel a heaviness you did not initially experience. What is happening is that the surrounding frequencies are trying to connect with you and instill the heaviness of the environment onto you.

If that person is sad or depressed, the frequencies within the room are transmitting those same emotions onto you as well. It is the same as when you encounter a space of vibrancy and tranquility—these same frequencies can impact your mood for the better.

Every second, minute, hour or day connections are being made. Sometimes instead of connecting as intended, the frequencies of the other person within the environment may or may not impact your frequency or you them. When you find you are feeling uncomfortable in various types of environments, think about your self-talk. Don't allow yourself to be influenced by the transmission of the environment.

Your efforts should always be on maintaining positive thoughts and high frequencies when entering into different environments. Whenever you find yourself encountering a low environment trace back to how you got there? Are you remaining open, letting go of your preconceived notions and embracing those that are different? Or are you being judgmental, experiencing discomfort of your own or through the transmission of others?

After you have performed this self-assessment, focus on getting back to your positive spectrum. Focus less on them and more on yourself until you are healthy enough to maintain your frequency. Much like any addiction, in order to fully recover you have to take the steps necessary to take care of yourself. Self care and awareness is key! You can tackle what is challenging you regardless of the environment.

Stop, reflect, and make the necessary adjustments by looking at how you communicate, beginning with your self-talk. It is crucial that you are purposeful when starting your day, morning, noon or night. This is what sets the pace for how we transmit our frequency throughout the day and how it is received by others.

Another surefire way to start your day is to begin with powerful affirmations. According to *Wikipedia,* affirmation displays a practice of positive thinking and self-empowerment which creates an achievement of success. Practice is the key to all things.

IAM!...
Loved
Whole
Understood

When you practice something, you are taking conscious, continual, and purposeful actions. You are creating a ritual. Proverbs 23:7 says "As a man thinks in his heart so is he." How are your thoughts being transmitted when you wake up? Reject any thoughts that transmit feelings of depression, unhappiness or anything that causes you to respond in an unflattering light to those that you encounter.

On occasion you may need to stop, meditate, journal or pray if you begin to feel overwhelmed. It is important to do this exercise after each phone call; meeting or any encounter that you have that stimulates a low frequency. This simple exercise will cause your frequency to adjust and be placed back into its positive alignment before heading off to the next task.

It may be painful to perform this self-reflection or to make this type of adjustment because you must be transparent and honest with yourself which doesn't always feel the best. It can be extremely difficult and frustrating, especially when you are dealing with others who may seem comfortable with where they are and not willing to do the work. But understand everyone isn't as motivated as you are to grow and practice self-work. All you can do is maintain your self-work and hope to be an example.

Eventually, if this form of self care through self-work does not catch on with your peers then it is quite possible that your relationship will inevitably fade due to having continually different frequencies. There are times that we do not wish to believe that we are being judgmental or have biases against someone, but we all have a trace of bias. As you transmit energy through your color frequency, look at ways to shape and adjust yourself.

Continue the process and make adjustments as needed in order to become a better communicator and to obtain optimal results. In performing self-work exercises, you must look at the man in the mirror. This can be challenging, sometimes you are willing to do the work, while other times you choose not to.

As you encounter others and you begin to see defense mechanisms surface either within them or yourself, remember that the only person that you can influence and change, is you. Be patient with yourself. You may not see results immediately because it takes a while to make the necessary adjustments to frequencies that have been living within you for so long.

You may begin to notice that as you perform your own self-work and effectively transform how you operate you become an example for others without realizing it. This type of response is human nature and a part of how leaders are formed. People tend to follow those they view as leaders and leadership takes on numerous forms.

Hurt People Hurt People

As the saying goes, "Hurt people hurt people." It is within these episodes of hurt that people begin to execute what they are feeling inside towards others. One's inability to organically connect and communicate causes issues that hinder growth.

So where and how does this breakdown in communication begin? The breakdown begins to transform during our childhood and then transitions into our teenage years. If nothing changes, the issues are not being recognized, and help is not sought, these experiences began to shape us into who we are as adults.

As was previously mentioned, during childhood your nature and how you were nurtured play a huge part not only in connection with your color frequency but in how you transmit information through frequency. As you transition into your teenage years, issues that were experienced during your childhood begin to collectively surface and impact your original frequency. These issues can include the lack of inclusivity, diversity biases, Isms, coupled with other issues encountered in your teenage years such as peer pressure, making life decisions, gender identity, understanding what love is, and self-image.

Everything we go through as a youth can greatly impact us. How low frequencies impact us look like forms of illness, including mental illnesses such as anxiety and depression or Post Traumatic Stress Disorder (PTSD). In the case of mental illness and PTSD, people run the risk of having a difficult time either being understood or understanding others.

According to *WebMD*, mental illness can be caused by several factors:

~: Biological;

~: Psychological; and

~: Environmental

According to the *Mayo Clinic*, PTSD can be the result of a traumatic event. Our environment and the things that we choose to mentally entertain can greatly impact and influence our emotions, thoughts, and behavior. Most times instead of fully dealing with an issue, we tend to move on with life and never address the problem until the low frequency experience surfaces in our lives, our relationships and impact the future.

EXAMPLE

Let's review how these illnesses can show up:

~: *Social media is causing information to be seen quicker; it creates an in-your-face approach to what is happening in the world that can make a person feel inadequate.*

~: *The number of shootings we hear about in the media started increasing greatly about 20 years ago when teenagers began to feel more like social outcasts due to not being accepted, lacking self-image, or experiencing the lack of love.*

~: *Children experiencing poverty in neighborhoods on a daily basis have no choice but to live in danger with little to no provisions, peace or outlets.*

~: *A dangerous pandemic sweeps across our country, death is saturating our community and no one is really aware of the root issue, the cure and its impact.*

~: *Individuals are being targeted and sometimes killed due to the color of their skin.*

All of these are examples of low frequencies that impact people that can show up as a form of illness from mental, anxiety, and depression to PTSD. If there is no support, professional help, or mentors to talk to, the youth tend to carry those wounds into adulthood, which greatly affects how they try to connect and communicate with others. What we are experiencing in the world around us, at our schools, workplace or places of worship, what we hear or see in the media, or the internet, greatly impacts and influences our frequency as well.

This is why daily affirmation is crucial before you start your day because lower frequencies are awaiting you if you are not prepared to ward them off. Whether you frequently experience high or low frequencies, it is important to understand that without effort we can often become our environment.

When TRANSMITTING, you must begin to take part in embracing, and influencing high frequencies. As a part of the shaping process, if people are experiencing feelings of isolation, depression, sadness, envy, hurt, despair, disappointment, jealousy, or suicidal thoughts we see the residue in these emotions when trying to make a connection. If a person is operating solely out of low frequencies you will begin to see why people hurt others due to their own internal hurts.

While technology is at an all-time high, people are becoming unhappier because these tools remove the essence of not only communication and connection but are creating a lack of closeness, unity and community. It is easy to go through a day teleworking, getting food and groceries delivered, and dating, all done virtually at any given time, and never experiencing any true personal interaction. While these new technologies are not bad, it does create a crutch for people to create a wall and become non-communicative, creating an unfriendly or standoffish behavior.

When people are confronted with uncertain conditions some express their true feelings through fear, pessimism, and panic. All of these changes are affecting and influencing how our color frequencies are interacting and being exchanged. With the increase of anti-social behaviors, people are unable to speak with each other in a safe and cohesive manner, which is causing a tremendous breakdown in communication.

It also appears that we are beginning to lack in cognitive abilities, i.e., common sense. A lack of cognitive skills influences us in many ways, starting with our communication and connection abilities. Test this theory for yourself. The next time you are at a cafe, restaurant, or, on public transportation, listen for silence. If you take a look around, you may notice that most people are tuned into their electronic devices.

This is the new way of communicating and connecting, some people tune in to these devices while communing with others—without actually speaking. If you pay close attention you will see them laughing or smiling at each other as they text and share pictures or messages through their devices. Connecting is important regardless of the format but personal interaction is the goal because it keeps our cognitive abilities sharpened.

As you try to connect make sure that your color frequencies intermingle effectively. People are hurting, and the lack of communication and connection only deepens that hurt. At the opening of the movie "Crash," a statement was made that displays how unconnected we have become.

> *In any real city, you walk, you brush past people, and people bump into you. In L.A. nobody touches you .... I think we miss that touch so much that we crash into each other just so we can feel something.*

~Crash, 2004, Wikiquote

When our conversations begin to become marked, tainted and scarred it is being introduced to toxic filter frequencies. We should try to avoid these low frequencies as soon as it is introduced, because they can influence the outcome of our communication styles. The key is to trace when the toxic filter was introduced into the conversation.

While it is something to be avoided, we should not be easily offended because this low frequency is coming from a person with experiences from their environment or past that has not been healed. This response can happen due to triggers within them that they have not dealt with, from diversity biases and lack of diversity, to Isms that have occurred.

Toxic Filter Frequencies Are Real

Don't allow toxic frequencies of others to transfer to you, it can cause you to become who they are.

~Vernita Naylor

Toxic frequencies are the lens in which we begin to view the world in a twisted fashion. It is within our hurts and disappointments that these toxic frequencies are centered. These toxic frequencies tend to show up in colors of white, gray, and black.

Initially, everything starts out within the positive spectrum, but then, as things begin to get worse, especially our self-talk or our interaction within a low frequency atmosphere; it transitions from white and gray to shades of black, depending upon the severity of the impact that is being felt. If the lack of making a conscious effort is not executed, and low frequencies begin to enter into your space, then a breakdown in communication occurs. Here is what these toxic frequencies represent when operating in the low frequency spectrum arena:

- WHITE–disinterested, cold, or uninviting
- GRAY–indecisive and emotionally detached
- BLACK–demanding, dominating, and intimidating

When these filters intertwine with your original color frequencies, they begin to dilute and overshadow your frequency and attach cold, uninviting, dominating, intimidating, and detached traits. If embraced, these frequencies can in turn translate into feelings of isolation, hurt, separation, bitterness, or lack of cohesiveness in connecting. Coupling these toxic filter frequencies with your original color frequencies causes a transmission of low feelings that emit hate, violence, or anger.

These low feelings then show up in our communication, and, at times, even physically.

EXAMPLE

When you have to work with a person you do not accept due to your Isms (or biases), you begin to transition from your original color frequency to embracing the toxic filter frequency of White, causing you to appear cold and uninviting.

As you continue interacting with people, and don't change how you think about them, your frequency transitions to Gray, causing feelings of detachment which begin to overtake you, further worsening your original color frequency. You may begin to feel isolated, unable to look at them or dread speaking with them. If you do not change your color frequency, your perspective will channel to Black, which causes intimidation.

At this point you might create a hindrance or hatred in your working relationships where you are so out of your element that you don't even recognize yourself.

According to *Wikipedia*, "hatred" is displayed by feelings of anger, disgust, and disposition towards the source, resulting in some form of hostility. Did you know there are different levels of hate, ranging from temporary to ingrained? Professor of Human Development Robert J. Sternberg (Cornell University), psychologist and psychometrician, analysis is that 'mutinous hatred' is a form of break down in communication when an individual or group refuses to associate with others. He indicates that there are three essential elements involved in hatred:

~: Negation of Intimacy

~: Passion

~: Devaluation

This form of communication can occur because we each have triggers that both affect and influence us in several ways. During these triggers you may have noticed that people make comments about how you are or have been behaving lately. Sometimes, it can even become an obstacle in your performance. Do these patterns and the statements being made sound familiar to you?

When you communicate in this fashion, you will be able to see how toxicity begins to overshadow the truth of who you truly are, how it creates an inability to accept what others bring to the table, or the inability to embrace others with gratitude, love, gratefulness, and acceptance. When we begin to feel stagnant and unhappy, feelings of prejudice, bitterness and loathing surface from deep within that eventually bubbles to the surface.

EXAMPLE

People that work in jobs that are meant to serve and protect, may experience low frequencies that tend to overtake the individuals negatively, causing them to get demoted, suspended, or lose their job due to their actions towards these individuals.

You will discover these toxic frequencies appearing whether it is with other individuals or within a group you are encountering. These changes not only affect the view of things, but they affect your perspective of others and the process of the intended message. These behaviors can be transmitted in various environments, including where a person should feel the safest.

It is important to be mindful as to how we are emitting frequencies, if this continues to happen; our communication effectiveness in obtaining the results we desire becomes greatly hindered. If you notice that you are continually not getting the results you desire, begin to reflect on why. In order to become successful in your communication practice, you must make a concentrated effort to *never* let your own negativity or that of others taint your original color frequency.

If you do not correct these low frequencies, during periods of hurt and despair, you begin to execute these hurt feelings toward not only yourself but others. This is when our communication frequencies can become tainted and at times dangerous. You may notice that during a conversation harmful words or hurtful actions are being exchanged. What this means is that during this conversation, we are actually speaking to the hurt or past of someone that may not involve the person or group that we're actually interacting with.

Connecting with someone who is not only different from you but someone you believed you knew all about can become eye opening and rewarding if you give it a chance. Toxic frequencies are real and should be taken seriously. Using the scientific experiment of John Vincent's Rice Consciousness Experiment, inspired by Dr. Maseru Emoto will help to further drive the point home about the impact of toxic filter frequencies. (See the video on YouTube at https://youtu.be/31shlv5Z71A)

In this experiment some cooked rice—about a teaspoon—was placed into two, separate, small, empty glass containers with lids. One container was labeled "love" and the other "hate." For five days, John exuded "love" and "hate" toward the perspective jars for 15 to 20 seconds each day.

The "hate" jar began to display evidence of mold, and every day thereafter, mold began to break down the rice considerably, while the "love" jar remained the same as it had originally started. On day nine it was evident that the mold in the "hate" jar had made an impact and had overtaken the rice. On day 13 the mold in the "hate" jar was so bad that liquid was settling on the bottom of the container while the "love" jar remained consistent. For more on John Vincent's Rice Consciousness Experiment, visit www.hypnosis.land and https://www.johnvincent.tv/

Rice
Experiment

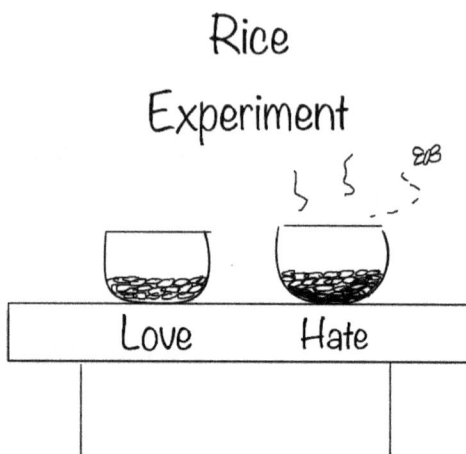

This experiment indicates "the impact of consciousness on reality," further illustrating the effects on a person subconsciously when you have either high or low frequency thoughts that are being directed towards you or what you say to yourself. As you can see, words and how they are transmitted are essential in your communication outcome. This is especially true if you or the other party is already experiencing some internal toxic frequencies prior to a conversation.

It is important to monitor your communication frequency whether you are a doctor, medical staff treating a patient, working on a construction project with other team members, working in law enforcement in a perceived hostile environment, or whatever the situation, what is being said, implied, or reacted to and how it is being transmitted can greatly impact the outcome.

Frequencies In Balance

Negativity is toxic and can spread like a virus, but with preventive care in how you think and what you speak, you can begin the healing process and balance your color frequency.

~Vernita Naylor

In order to become an effective communicator, you must be able to create a positive connection, especially in order to obtain the desired results or goals that you are seeking. During ineffective communication, your nurture frequency, that was once innate and so special to your being and in whom you are, has become tainted with toxic frequencies. When your color frequencies are tainted in low self-esteem, low life experiences, Isms or biases, it can alter who you originally were and how you originally communicate.

Low frequencies affect some people so deeply that instead of creating a barrier to combat the frequencies it begins to transition and settle within them. This settlement of low frequencies begins to become a part of who they are; it becomes a part of their actions and in how they connect with others. The irony is that these toxic frequencies begin to seem normal to the individual.

It becomes so normal that the individual tends to believe it is others who are out of sync rather than themselves. These toxic frequencies begin to continually dilute communication flow and starts to transition from the white to the gray and if not corrected then overshadow to the black filter frequency. As previously stated when your filters turn to black you are severely out of balance.

EXAMPLE

During this phase, most biases (or Isms) take a seat within the heart and influence our actions. When you live in this space you discover that matching energy occurs when you can't find your keys, you have a flat tire, someone took the parking space you were patiently waiting for, everyone is moving slowly in the lunch rush, and on your way home you are stuck in traffic

These are examples of remaining in low filter frequencies. If you allow this to happen it is possible that you will continue this energy and become extremely exhausted and tired. For some, that refuse to look within tend to blame others for what is happening around them. As you are operating within this low spectrum, the only way to color correct is to stop and tap into how you got there, why you are feeling this way, and what you should do to reprogram your mind.

The goal is to at least get back to the mid-spectrum range and eventually higher frequency. Always be mindful of your actions, behavior, demeanor, and emotions, especially if you are a leader in any capacity. How you react to any occurrence determines the outcome.

If there are low frequencies in your leadership approach then it can be contagious, and can affect your team in a negative manner resulting in non-positive results. As you lead, the team follows.

All Abuse Is Toxic

Fear is the memory of pain. Addiction is the memory of pleasure. Freedom is beyond both.

~Deepak Chopra

When TRANSMITTING frequencies, it is always essential to keep the betterment of the results or goals to be accomplished at the forefront. The goal is to make the process as smooth as possible, with minimal intrusion, hurt, harm, or danger. Staying within the positive spectrum of our color frequency, will help to continue to garner desired results but if you remain within the toxic spectrum it can be deadly.

You may not realize it, but a person may not be operating with a biased attitude but rather living with a broken one. This brokenness can occur due to something that happened in their lives from childhood, to adulthood. Whatever occurred in their lives can take on the form of abuse from psychological to physical.

The *National Domestic Violence Hotline* states that domestic violence does not discriminate. Anyone of any race, age, sexual orientation, religion, or gender, regardless of whether they are married, living together, dating, or within any socioeconomic or educational background or level can be a victim or perpetrator of domestic violence. Domestic violence includes physical and/or psychological harm, arouses fear, prevents a person from doing what they wish or forces them to behave in ways they do not want. Domestic violence takes on several forms of behavior, just like with substance and alcohol abuse. If you are being abused call 1-800-799-SAFE (7233) or for more information, visit www.thehotline.org.

According to the *Mayo Clinic*, substance abuse, also known as drug abuse, can interfere with one's health, work, or social relationships. Drug abuse can take the form of recreational drugs, like marijuana, or illegal narcotics causing the same type of disruption of life. A lot of people ask the question as to whether prescription drugs can create the same form of adverse affect as substance or drug abuse?

In today's society, opioid addiction is at an all-time high. While opioids are effective for treating pain, they can also be highly addictive just like the affects of substance abuse. Opioids like OxyContin, Vicodin, and morphine are considered the pain relievers of choice for many people. Opioids create an addictive chemical response in some brains, causing many Americans to become hooked.

People are different and react to these drugs in numerous ways; it all depends upon how the brain reacts to the drugs. According to the *American Psychiatric Association* (www.psychiatry.org), there are approximately over two million people within the U.S. who have a substance abuse disorder related to opioid prescription medication. While the U.S Department of Health and Human Services (HHS) estimates that in the U.S. over 2.1 million people struggle with opiods.

Opioid overdose deaths have increased rapidly. Of those prescribed with this medication, the number of overdose deaths have doubled since 2010 from 21,000 to more than 42,000 in 2016. Regardless, of the type of abuse, people in this position may not know how to clearly deal with the abuse or bias they've experienced, so they begin to internalize it and at times begin to blame themselves and believe that they deserve this treatment.

As people begin to internalize, the substance, physical, or psychological abuse it can also become an addictive behavior. Just like someone operating in a rage or bullying behavior, a person internalizing abuse can be difficult to communicate with as well. This person may seem unmotivated, withdrawn, unable to focus on what is being said, or experiencing the inability to complete a task as promised.

Bias, just like abuse, can operate in a toxic form. Nothing is to be taken lightly when abuse is at the forefront, because while initially, it can seem to be light, it can eventually turn into something askewed and heavy between all parties involved. You will hear that people do not have control over alcohol or drug abuse because it is considered a disease that affects the brain. Can this also be said about biases or Isms? In understanding abuse and the various forms it can take will assist you in having a clearer understanding of the toxicity that surrounds you and how to avoid these frequencies attaching to you.

Understanding not only yourself but others will help you become extremely effective. Embrace the new opportunity that has been presented to you. Learn who you are then you will be in a much better position to understand and connect with others.

To Thine Own Self Be True.

~William Shakespeare (Hamlet)

All In The Family

In being a part of a family we tend to believe what they say, what we hear and that their behavior is normal, until we begin to experience more of the outside world.

In order to improve who you are, especially if you are exhibiting excessive toxic frequencies, think about the root of the toxicity and where it comes from. As you begin to search within yourself and be honest about who you've become you will begin to reflect and realize that there is a lot of hard work ahead of you that needs to be undone.

In order to undo low frequencies originally occuring in childhood, the process must be worked backwards. It may sound confusing, but actually, it is simple if you are consciously aware of it. This is how the backwards process works.

Dig deeper, look at, discover and trace the essence of your feelings, behavior and why you're communicating in the way that you are. Stop and ask yourself, how was your childhood? What did your past look like? How has it influenced your present and future behavior?

By taking a look at your childhood, you may see some patterns in how you communicate. Do you recall how your family communicated and the style in which they did so? As a child, was your voice being heard, were you continually misunderstood, or felt invisible?

For some, during their childhood, they may have experienced parents or a guardian who were abusive due to alcohol, medication, or illegal drug usage, and the abuse was pushed onto the child, either physically or psychologically. Or you may have experienced watching or hearing frequent biases (or Isms) in the form of racism, sexism, classism, ableism, or ageism to name a few.

Is this what has caused you to become withdrawn, lack motivation, bully others, live in fear, intimidated by others, or _____? (You fill in the blank.) Take a closer look at how your past influenced your future. As you reflect, do you see anything that resembles some of the low frequency aspects of what you were exposed to in your early environment? You may ask why looking into your past is so important?

Looking into your past allows you the ability to truly see how you arrived at where you are. Your past dictates and shapes your future—unless you make some changes. Your past is where your communication style was formed; it begins in early childhood and is then shaped into your adulthood.

EXAMPLE

Were you raised in an animated home with shouting and aggressive behavior; or a loving home with words of affirmation, hugs, support and kisses; or surrounded by people who expressed themselves through passive aggression? These various forms of communication are what we as children tend to adapt to in forming our own level of communication styles, in most cases, well into adulthood.

Childhood is a time when we should feel safe, supported, and be prepared for the world. Children are dreamers, adaptable, flexible and tend to block things out due to their need for survival, love, and support. Children are curious risk takers, and for them there is always something new and wonderful to discover about someone or something different.

As a child you believe that you can do anything and dream big. Remember when you thought you could fly off the roof because you saw your favorite hero do the same? Or what about when you believed you could make something that you loved that you believed others would want to have or buy?

In our teenage years is the time when we begin to work on making our dreams a reality but this is also the time where those that should love and support us say "stop dreaming," "you can't do that" or "if you build that and try to sell it no one will buy it." At this point as teenagers we begin to move away from taking risks and discovering new things and people due to our experiences of the hurt feelings that has began to surface.

Gradually as these feelings and emotions begin to surface our perspective on how we view things and people tend to change as well. Then as an adult there are occasions when, during the times of our hurt, we begin to reflect on our upbringing and how we were raised which enhances the toxic frequencies brewing within us.

Our frequencies tend to attract various types of energy to us. The energy being transmitted attracts both high and low frequencies. We all give off and receive various forms of frequencies that can either be helpful or hurtful to us or those around us. If you ever find you are confused as to why, when you encounter certain people, they appear to be continually turned off, and tend to walk away from you, any of these could be one of the reasons.

To someone else your behavior could seem strange or abnormal, but to you everything is normal; this is how you were raised, this is your world. In the same fashion, they see their behavior as normal as well; it is how they were raised, this is their world. The goal here is to find a middle ground for achievement.

Until we begin to look more closely at how others communicate differently than how we were nurtured, or if we continue to discover that we lack the ability to obtain the results we desire, then we will continue to obtain the same result—miscommunication! If you find yourself experiencing toxic frequencies through your constant miscommunication could it be that when you are speaking to either an individual or a group, you are speaking according to your past hurts? Focus on changing the narrative by giving them and yourself a chance to experience a better level of communication. Begin to focus on trying to wholeheartedly take a different approach, open up and never assume that you know the stories of others, let them tell you their own story and be prepared to receive it.

You will be amazed by what new things you can learn through self-talk messaging, accepting, and embracing the change of being different.

Karma Is Real

People will forget what you said; people will forget what you did, but people will never forget how you made them feel.

~Maya Angelou

The words within this quote could never be truer because it is that feeling that determines so much, especially in how we communicate, connect, and work together. If people do not feel valued, they will let you know by exhibiting behavior that ranges from being reserved and uncooperative to becoming distant and difficult to work with.

EXAMPLE

When you are in a jovial mood, the Universe offers you more good things on that frequency, but in turn, when you are feeling negative, negativity is exactly what you will get in return. This is called karma.

Karma is real; you get what you give. According to *Wikipedia*, "karma" incites a cause-and-effect syndrome. It occurs as the result of a person's actions. Karma is a cycle of energy. Being transparent, getting to the root of your being, understanding why and how you are communicating is key.

Change, improvement, or altering the issues that are causing these toxic frequencies—depending on how deep they are-healing can take years to resolve and eradicate. Some people are unwilling to dig deeply and face their greatest fears in order to help reduce the time needed to heal. In order to make the necessary improvements, you must remain honest and be consistent in your efforts.

Honesty is the key when you begin to realize the type of toxic frequencies you are carrying and seeing within yourself. The results of changing the outcome when toxic frequencies are being introduced can be found within your conversations. Your conversations speak volumes to whether you are able to connect. How you speak, act, and what you do emits the karma that you disperse to others.

To improve your karma frequency, first, you must face how you are feeling; second, accept it; third, embrace it, and last, look at how to change it. Even with root causes or generational patterns, what you are experiencing can cause not only hurt but fear. When any process of change occurs, do not rush into it, but take it a step at a time to begin effective healing.

To assist in the process, some people may seek outside help from a psychologist, psychiatrist, group therapy sessions, friends and families or spiritual practices. Regardless of the process being used, getting to the root cause of the problem is the ultimate key to healing. This is why what's inside comes out and reflects in how you treat others.

TRANSMITTING ASSESSMENT: GOING DEEPER WITHIN YOURSELF

Part I: Challenge Yourself

This exercise is a two week process that reflects more on hearing, listening, and writing. Every time you are asked a question during this exercise, stop, listen, and address how you are feeling by reflecting on the question and then writing down your answer. Write your thoughts quickly, don't hesitate or ponder. Initially it is the first thoughts that are the right ones. You may not be clear about some things as you are TRANSMITTING through your frequency, but when you begin to write down what you heard, think or feel being transmitted things will become clearer. Be honest with yourself, no matter how painful it may seem, in order to grow and work through the transition:

1. When you encounter someone who is different or don't understand, how do you respond?

2. What types of frequencies were being transmitted within you when you encountered them? For example, are you operating within your original color frequency, or do you find yourself experiencing toxic frequencies when you either see them or hear their voice?

3. If you discover that you are experiencing toxic frequencies, describe which stage you are operating in. (Hint: white, gray, or black spectrum.)

4. Why? How did you get there?

5. Go deeper. What are you saying to yourself about them?

6. Is it them or is it you with the issue?

7. Was this an initial response, or was it a gradual occurrence?

8. When did this reaction occur?

9. Did anything change over the course of the conversation, whether it was a 30-second or 30-minute conversation?

10. How are you feeling? Anxious, rejection, frustration, shame, fear, heard, joyful_____ (fill in the blank)

11. How do you believe that this conversation could be improved?

Regardless of how you feel, especially if it is a low frequency, imagine as you speak with people to reflect on the words that are being transmitted. Visually begin to pay more attention to these words, as if you see them being transmitted in the air. Visualizing the words in color creates a more vivid illustration of what you are feeling.

Do you like what you see being transmitted through the words expressed? Do you like how the communication is going? How are you receiving the information the other person is TRANSMITTING? Focus on making the necessary adjustments towards the positive spectrum.

As you continue this process you will begin to see improvement in your communication style. As you continue to improve, not only will you notice the change, but others will begin to notice it as well. Each week continue this process and compare what you see.

Part II: What Does Your Analysis Chart Say?

This exercise is a two week process that reflects on not staying on the surface but to go deeper. It is important to analyze your conversations using the following information:

1. Write a synopsis of your last low (negative) frequency conversation and then do the same for a positive conversation written separately.

2. Outline the pros and cons of what you felt being transmitted in each conversation.

3. Analyze what you see.

4. Walk away from what you've written and let it immerse into your being.

5. In the positive conversation did you feel included or embraced? In the low conversation did you feel rejection or isolation? If so, why or why not?

It is important how you answer the above-mentioned

questions because the answers will show whether you are able to accept someone outside yourself. You will notice in your analysis what is missing, what needs to be added, or what needs to improve in your communication. When you find that you are continuously not getting the desired results work through this exercise periodically until you see the improvement.

To obtain the ultimate results, you must be honest with yourself that progress is being made, even if the progress is small. STAY THE COURSE. It can be frustrating to work on improving a 'life learned trait.'

Part III: Dig Deep Within Yourself

This exercise is a one week process that reflects on continuing your communication growth. You will begin to see how you interact in TRANSMITTING your frequency. When frequencies are being exchanged organically and fluidly, communication can become successful.

If allowance is not present when trying to connect, it can cause a breakdown. As you dig deeper write down how the following impacts you to better understand yourself:

~: What toxic frequencies are you still holding on to?

~: Why do you appear to continually be operating within the mid-to-low spectrum?

~: What is your perception of your journey so far? How does and has it influenced your communication style?

If people do not connect, the energy begins to become tainted, and communication breaks down. This breakdown creates a cloud of confusion and misunderstanding. As colors do, we can all bind and work together if we try. Our colors not only represent our personalities, behavior, and character traits, they also represent our diversity.

It is diversity that we bring to the table when communicating with one another and that can create either low or high frequency energy. This energy creates enlightenment, ideas and creativity as well as fluid and unique approaches to various methods in communicating.

Part IV: Always Challenge Yourself

Always look for ways to challenge yourself. When you communicate with individuals write down how you honestly feel. In order to be effective in determining whether you are meeting or obtaining your desired results, you need to see yourself from a 4-D perspective, which means to see yourself from all sides including top to bottom. Be honest as you look at what are the key factors in the collective breakdown or success in your communication.

EXAMPLE

Imagine you are a manager that has a project that needed to be completed by a certain date. Despite your efforts you and your team did not meet your goal. Clearly define what happened that caused this mishap. Next, determine what the necessary steps would be for improvement and to reach your goal the next time especially if you are working with the 'same' team.

Take small steps by continuing the practice until you reach your set goals. As you continue to view yourself in different situations and circumstances, you will discover various outcomes. In some ways you may be thriving and getting some great results, but there could be other situations or circumstances that are lacking.

Reflect on and write what you see about yourself and others during these times. You will be amazed at what you discover. Remember, honesty is the key during this exercise.

Let's take it a step further in challenging yourself. The next time you see someone or speak to someone, especially those you perceive to be different look for how you can connect without being insulting or passing judgment. Not only listen to what is being said but pay attention to body language.

As you continue to journal your experiences, you will notice that the more you practice the *Speaking in Colors* concept, the better you will become in communicating and connecting. Remember, we each come with different personalities, and this is what reflects diversity. Always look forward to learning something new and different about others. You can't change them, but you can change your response towards them.

You can connect by being present in the moment. Share and learn the story of others. Let's continue to consciously change how we think and feel about each other. You will be amazed at the perspective of someone else and what they have to say.

Remember, when communicating, everyone should feel embraced, feel safe, and have their voice heard. This is what the *Speaking in Colors* concept teaches and what it is all about.

FOURTH COLOR FREQUENCY:
COLOR CORRECTION

Color Correction Is A Slow Process

As you focus on color correcting, know that it will be a slow process. When you decide to change your perspective, it can be life changing. In your journey of trauma, inconveniences, and discord, whether within your childhood, teenage years, or adulthood, you need to realize that, in order to live a more cohesive and fluid life, you must change yourself from within.

Using the *Speaking in Colors* concept makes COLOR CORRECTION simple. It can be performed easily if you take the time to try the process. You can change everything by incorporating this process but it must begin with you and only you.

What is the COLOR CORRECTION process? It is the steps required to correct the original origin of your frequencies that is responsible for low connection outcomes and their influences. If you want to improve and gain the results you desire, you must first change what is in your mind.

As you begin to master COLOR CORRECTION, you begin to transition and use the information in connecting with others. In operating your frequency through the spectrum, it is your perception and your interaction with others that determine the outcome during communication.

EXAMPLE

Imagine you woke up today and found yourself operating within the mid to low spectrum because you did not sleep as well as you expected. You did not work to elevate your frequency nor did you consider the possibilities of what external or internal influences that could affect your day.

As you walk into a meeting, you meet the team you are to work with. Among the five team members, you discover there are a few who you are familiar with from being unmotivated, and lack interest to a few cooperating. What do you do?

In order to color correct properly you must first gauge your behavior by performing a self-check. Next, perform an honest evaluation of what is currently happening within the atmosphere. Lastly, by knowing what your spectrum was when entering the room you can begin to make a paradigm shift in how to properly respond to others when the situation or circumstance arises again.

You must do this despite how you are feeling, what you believe or have heard about the others that are on your team. Look at the behaviors of everyone on your team. Are there any external forces that are impacting and influencing the energy surrounding you? Did others come to work without doing their self-check?

Remind yourself that regardless of the temperature of the room you must work together, and tap into your positive spectrum continually. As the leader you must positively influence the temperature of the room by leading by example. Your attitude in how you lead and guide the group, makes a bigger difference than you can imagine. If you find yourself being swayed between the high and low aspects of your original frequency, try to remain steady.

It is important to develop a positive mantra of encouragement and motivation that you can use to repeat to yourself as often as necessary to stay uplifted. When negativity tries to rule the outcome of the team show others that you can change the message of what you are receiving by sending positive frequencies. Even when something unsettling happens, do not deny it. Accept it and then correct it.

You must maintain the necessary frequency to impact and influence the outcome. Here are some quick steps to help you understand how to effectively color correct and gain a better understanding of how to obtain the results you desire:

- ~: There must be a safe place for everyone's voices to be heard, and it begins with you. You must create that safe place.

- ~: When you are speaking with someone stay focused on what is being said and less of what you are saying or thinking about that person.

- ~: To assure that you fully understand the message, repeat back to the person what you believe you heard, this helps to remove your perceptive hearing to gain clarity.

- ~: Ask the person to repeat, in their own words, what they believe you are saying, it helps to eliminate any further misunderstanding.

- ~: Gauge the results by determining whether you are on point or missing vital information while performing a self-check to understanding why.

- ~: Ask yourself what caused the breakdown? Was it them, you, or the collective?

These steps will help you make sure that information is being exchanged correctly while minimizing misunderstanding. As you continue this process, you will get better in TRANSMITTING and exchanging your frequency and information. Additionally, this process will help you be able to gauge your level of understanding and that of others.

The key is to take your time and not get frustrated in the process. Each day evaluate what is your initial frequency and what frequencies will you allow to accept and influence you. You can always color correct by mentally starting from where you are.

Take note of what you are feeling and concentrate on a positive affirmation. Every day and throughout the day repeat your affirmation to maintain your balance. This is especially essential if you are off-balance because you would need to perform this exercise daily until you discover the change within.

If today were your last day, how would you live it? Would you stoop to the low level frequencies of others or would you remain in your high frequency? Do not become fixated on changing the frequency of others, because there are some who may not respond as you wish. You can impact others by your consistent example. Live in the moment, as if it were your last.

Toxic Behavior Is Not Normal

Some people are in such utter darkness that they will burn you just to see a light. Try not to take it personally.

~Kamand Kojouri

People begin to see toxic frequencies as a normal part of their being, which can become a subtle obstacle within their lives in several ways. When we are continuously operating in toxicity, it appears to be normal. We become confused as to why we have trouble connecting with others without realizing it is us and our behavior or interaction with them. How we deal with these unsettling circumstances helps to determine the ultimate outcome.

If you want to see changes, you need to begin to create a paradigm shift. You make this paradigm shift by beginning to see toxic behavior for what they are, unhealthy. Do not accept toxicity as a normal way of behaving.

EXAMPLE

If someone is continually talking at you, down to you, or in an animated way within one to two feet of your personal space, do not treat this as normal behavior, especially if you feel intimidated or uncomfortable. These feelings may not affect you directly or immediately, but if you feel even slightly threatened, it is not an acceptable behavior.

When you are experiencing these types of toxic frequencies from others, the goal is to consciously make intentional steps toward progress, first recognizing it and then stopping it. Toxicity can be subtle, and may appear to be normal. The reason why some people may not initially see toxicity either within themselves or others is because it can show up in several ways:

~: Mentally

~: Verbally

~: Physically

The process of color correcting comes when you are able to recognize the toxic behavior, either within yourself or from others. You will discover that just because you are choosing to evolve, everyone is not ready to do the same. Instead of concentrating on what is happening, focus on yourself and do your own self work. As you know, it is hard to change a behavior that has been with you for most of your life; it is the same with others.

Let's look at toxicity as a form of pregnancy. During pregnancy, the woman is formulating the child within her womb. This is the time when everything is created, from the brain and limbs to the baby's innate abilities. Once this child is born, it has its own behavior patterns, some of which will be influenced by the child's upbringing.

Overall, the child's life and environment helps to set and regulate the stage of how this child will interact with the world around them. This is the same with toxicity, at birth, it begins to take root and establish behavior patterns which can range from mentally and verbally to physically. Just as the child, the toxicity react naturally, habitually, and consistently. If these patterns are not improved the root that has become a part of our brain's natural responses at birth begins to appear normal well into our adulthood.

It has been stated that people tend to focus more on the low (negative) frequency than the high spectrum. Hara Estroff Mariano, in the *Psychology Today* article "Our Brain's Negative Bias: Why Our Brains Are More Highly Attuned to Negative News," states: "Nastiness just makes a bigger impact on our brains. And that is due to the brain's "negativity bias." Your brain is simply built with a greater sensitivity to unpleasant news. The bias is so automatic that it can be detected at the earliest stage of the brain's information processing."
Source: https://www.psychologytoday.com/us/articles/200306/our-brains-negative-bias, June 20, 2003, updated June 9, 2016

We don't see things as they are; we see them as we are.

~Anais Nin

During various levels of toxicity our internal veil begins to see life through distorted lens. There are times when this veil is based upon reality and other times based upon our perceptions, and what we see as real. This can be due to behaviors of prejudice or bias that have been inflicted upon us.

In fact it is all of these things that we physiologically or psychologically omit within ourselves, oftentimes without being aware. This behavior must change. After a while we begin to learn how to mask ourselves, which becomes a part of who we are. We perform this act because we prefer not to face the uncomfortable part of ourselves that has been hurt or wounded.

We act in the same way when we prefer not to accept this behavior from others.

EXAMPLE

If we have a loved one who is addicted to drugs or alcohol, we tend to excuse them and act as if their behavior is not really what we or others see. We also tend to excuse their behavior toward others, even when they behave badly.

Excusing any type of toxic behavior is unacceptable. One day you will wake up and realize that all of this time you have been violated by this behavior of toxicity that has now been internalized and impacting your life.

Stop the toxic frequency influences on your life now.

You cannot change the behavior of others, but you can change your behavior and your response to others. Things will not improve if you do not focus and work on yourself first. Don't worry about others and their lack of motivation or participation as you focus on color correcting.

Patience Is A Process

*Patience is not simply the ability to wait—
it's how we behave while we're waiting.*

~Joyce Meyers

When trying to learn how to be an effective communicator, the goal is patience. You must not only be patient with yourself but patient with others, while exercising a spirit of forgiveness, release, and openness. You recognize that you are not operating in a spirit of forgiveness, release, or openness by your behavior when interacting.

This happens when you encounter an individual you believe has hurt or wronged you; it is your behavior towards that person that reflects and provides an indication of how you actually feel.

EXAMPLE

Imagine that you enter a room and encounter a person you feel has wronged you. You notice that you begin to experience some type of discomfort and are emitting patterns of toxic frequencies. This indicates that you have not forgiven this person.

This discomfort can encompass several behavior patterns:

- ~: Isolation
- ~: Separation
- ~: Suppression
- ~: Oppression
- ~: Extremely Introverted or Extroverted Behavior
- ~: Excessive Feelings of Inferiority or Superiority
- ~: Emotional Imbalance
- ~: Overconfidence
- ~: Anger
- ~: Withdrawal
- ~: Self-Entitlement

However, if you encounter this individual or groups and you remain within your high color frequency then you are on your way to improvement and color correcting. These include:

~: Inclusion

~: Connection

~: Emotional Balance

~: Confidence

~: Welcoming

~: Harmony

Your emotional responses will help you to better understand whether you are on your way to acceptance, release, openness and forgiveness or not. If you are open enough to allow it, you will also discover that when meeting people, especially someone new, just like when you read a good book, you will discover something new and different about them each time you interact with them.

When frequencies emit an adverse reaction due to interacting with those we don't understand or feel misunderstood by, we are not giving color correcting a chance, and thus, we are unable to accomplish our goals or the task at hand. Some people tend to seek out communities that accept them as they are, but at times this too can become detrimental because it can keep them in a vulnerable position. While in these communities, you should be accepted, but it can also translate into other dangerous situations, causing people to question themselves even more.

Some of these communities include people who themselves are hurting, thus continuing the hurt.

EXAMPLE

In a church of any denomination, where people go for refuge, you will find a lot of hurt people where at times can hurt others, including you. Hurt people, hurt people. Despite how you choose to work through your healing process—alone, with a therapist, or among like-minded people—the work first begins with self, start now.

When you begin to incorporate self-improvement color-correcting techniques, things will be more inclusive for everyone involved. You do not need to accept anyone who is exuding hate toward you to understand that they are TRANSMITTING and operating in a toxic frequency. The ultimate factor here is to be patient with the process while realizing that others are operating based upon the toxic frequencies that have been placed upon them. The key is to acknowledge and not stoop to their level.

As religious author Yehuda Berg says:

Hurt people hurt people. That's how pain patterns get passed on, generation after generation after generation. Break the chain today. Meet anger with sympathy, contempt with compassion, and cruelty with kindness. Greet grimaces with smiles. Forgive and forget about finding fault. Love is the weapon of the future.

Healing Trauma And Working Towards Correction

Let no man pull you so low as to hate him.

~Martin Luther King Jr.

It can be hard to get past trauma, hurt, biases and the pain regardless of when it happened. For some it still feels like yesterday. If the impact was direct, and you were the victim of someone subjecting you to their toxic frequencies, whether it was on a frequent or infrequent basis, it can become surreal to deal with.

EXAMPLE

The impact can also be painful even if the impact is indirect. Perhaps you are aware of someone within your community or circle who you knew or saw was unfairly treated due to the toxic frequencies of others, can hurt deeply.

Whenever trauma occurs it usually causes a breakdown in communication and connecting. Ask yourself, "What are you seeing and saying to yourself that is causing the breakdown?" "What am I initially feeling?" Dig deep and take a look at your perspective. Has your perspective been molded by past looks, actions, conversations, or by something you are holding onto from your past? Are you directing this behavior or feelings to the proper individual, or should it be directed to someone else?

In order to correct the toxic frequencies that are plaguing us, and to begin the healing process, we all must make an effort to respond to these frequencies, whether it is within ourselves or in response to connecting with others. How we each handle trauma or the essence of life speaks to our uniqueness.

Our diversity is important because it allows us to exchanges ideas, information, and influences in ways that we may not have heard of or previously experienced. When exercising COLOR CORRECTION, it is essential that you take your Isms and your ego out of the conversation if you want to become a successful communicator. We are not our skin, our clothes, or our religion, and we all deserve to be given a chance to be heard.

While watching the movie *Invictus*, it was important to see that, regardless of the harsh treatment Nelson Mandela was subjected to, he was still able to find within himself some essence of forgiveness for those who wanted to imprison him for life. The poem "*Invictus*," by William Ernest Henley, was instrumental in helping Mandela keep his head above the chatter he experienced in the small cell during his 27-year incarceration. Despite the fact that he became the first black president of South Africa, after his release from prison he had to make a conscious effort to overcome prejudices, biases, and racism that he and the country were still living with in South Africa to be able to lead successfully.

Mandela was able to get past his personal trauma to color correct; he did not let the actions of others impact his future. The poem *"Invictus,"* among other things, was his affirmation or mantra in keeping himself focused toward his goals of forgiveness and ending the injustice plaguing the country. How Mandela handled the trauma may not be the pathway you wish to take, but you need to discover a way that works best for you for effective healing.

Getting past any type of trauma, hurt, or bias requires a necessary and continual conscious effort in order to move towards correction. Mandela was able to turn around the trauma, bias, and hurt he experienced to speak to the people of South Africa and to be heard. With the right method and process, you too can become a successful communicator and make an effective connection.

Creating A Safe Place For Expressing Your Frequency

When someone shows you who they are,
believe them the first time.

~Maya Angelou

Creating a place of safety is essential. People must have a safe place to retreat when they feel intimidated, overwhelmed or are operating in an unfamiliar territory. This will allow for more effective and open communication. This is one of the principles of color correcting.

When we begin to notice any disconnection within ourselves or others, we must admit it, own it and not deny the healing process. When toxic frequencies occur it can result in issues such as misunderstandings, shame, hurt or indifference. In communicating this can happen frequently, but to the untrained eye it may not be clear as to the reason why.

Let's explore some ways in which people may not feel as safe and where they may miss the subtle movement of being mistreated:

- ~: Passive-Aggressive
- ~: Talking over you
- ~: Being dismissive or ignoring you while you are talking

~: Argumentative

~: Operating too closely within your personal space without your permission

~: Not allowing the other person's voice to be heard

In trying to relate, we must be mindful and continue to remain within our high spectrum. If you focus on changing your own self-talk of indifference, how you connect and embrace others, things will change. By performing these steps, the process will help you begin to improve how you connect and how you view things, especially with those that remind you of your biases from the past.

By beginning to change the conversation in your mind and embracing others, you begin to remain within the high spectrum and also improve your own color frequencies while operating within your true self. Always look for ways to make sure you create a safe place for connecting, interacting and communicating with others. Look at how you can change and improve the conversation to obtain the results, and the outcome you desire.

If you are unsure of something, emulate a child. No matter what happens, children trust. Try trusting. When children feelings are hurt, they adjust. Try adjusting. When people don't show children the love they desire, the children embrace them anyway. Try embracing. Whenever children are curious about things, they ask questions. Never be afraid to ask questions. When they are looking for new experiences, children explore. Try exploring the newness of what is happening around you while you let go of your past fears. Try talking to someone about what you're feeling to help create balance.

The essence of a child is to seek safety and peace, especially in familiar surroundings. Everyone should be able to feel safe and have their voice heard. As you begin to see and understand what is happening, trust, adjust, embrace, ask, explore and let go. You will be able to fully color correct when you practice the essence of surrender.

The process can work if you take the time to work it, but you must be honest with yourself. You can also create a miserable life for yourself if you are judgmental and bias about yourself and others. Here are some examples of how judgment and biases can impact your life:

- ~: You are not promoted based on management's Isms on how you look, speak, or act

- ~: You are not heard or validated because your spouse wants you to agree with them and make them feel secure

- ~: You have created a blockage within yourself due to how you perceive your friends are treating you

~: You own a nice car and are continuously harassed by law enforcement due to the color of your skin

~: You are not called upon for certain social activities or employment due to your perceived age

~: You are not perceived to be a good parent due to your sexual preference

If people do not feel validated, they tend not to become a part of the process of growth and have no interest in working effectively with others for common goals. These biases or Isms causes distrust and affects everything that we do on a regular basis. If you notice that you are being heavily affected by these Isms then it is time for you to speak up.

Be clear about your boundaries and what is and is not acceptable in order to effectively co-exist. Our purpose on this earth is to share love and light not to dim our light or that of others.

If others see that you care, have empathy and are inclusive you can gain better results when connecting and communicating. People will be your champion if they feel valued, but first, operating in a safe place to overcome trauma is the key.

The Formula For Correcting Communication

If you are in a bad mood, go for a walk. If you are still in a bad mood, go for another walk.

~Hippocrates

Communication takes on different forms, from verbal to non-verbal, assertive to passive-aggressive. In order to be able to effectively communicate within your color frequency, you must take the time to work with others. At the same time, you must do this with the willingness to understand others, which can be a difficult and challenging task.

The essence of a conversation can be simple if you execute the right formula. Here is a simple formula for understanding the COLOR CORRECTION process:

$$\text{Sender's Color Frequency} + \text{Conveyed Message} + \text{Receiver's Frequency}$$

$$= \text{Communication Results} (+ \text{ Or } -)$$

EXAMPLE

Here is how to better understand this formula: When the behavior, character, or personality traits of Red (Empowerment) and Yellow (Mindfulness)—which are total opposites—communicate, they must operate within a spectrum that is cohesive to each other. In order to color correct the frequency, Orange must be present which represents a balance and cohesiveness between the two traits.

How did we arrive at this point? What does this means? During our formative years as children, we had the pleasure of mixing colors during art time. At this time we had fun being creative as we mixed various colors. We found out that mixing colors helped us to discover a whole new world. We discovered when you mixed red and yellow, we arrived at orange. It was at this formative stage we discovered that colors was one of the ways in how we communicate.

During this exciting phase, we were actually communicating by *Speaking in Colors* and did not even know it. The colors we chose to play with and work with not only attracted our emotions but reflected a part of ourselves. This process is the same type of process when mixing different personality, character, or behavior traits when interacting. As we come together each person come with their own traits. In order to get effective results each person must be prepared to have a meeting of the minds by operating within the high spectrum of their color frequency in making a connection. You may not know the color frequency of others but you must find a way to de-escalate the imbalance and neutralize the conversation for effective communication.

It is important to operate in a more cohesive manner to obtain the results that you desire. COLOR CORRECTION says that it's time to do some work. Utilize the power of your self control to neutralize and balance interactions that you have with others to acquire the optimal communication results. As you are working through this process be mindful of your thoughts. Remember, we often become what we think and speak.

How others react to us during communication determines if what we intended is exactly what we meant to convey or express. This is where we can determine if a connection was made and whether the COLOR CORRECTION process worked.

When TRANSMITTING frequencies, your intended message can be interpreted in low or high frequencies. While you may get a response, some of us do not yet understand why others respond or react to us the way in which they do. In these cases, when your results are not what you expect consider the following:

~: "Could it be something that I said or didn't say?"

~: "Was it the way I responded or did not respond?"

~: "How was my tone and body language?"

~: "Are my biases or Isms getting in the way?"

~: "Where they inflicting their biases or Isms on me?"

When we initially communicate we do not consider how we are TRANSMITTING, we should intentionally watch how we are interacting and connecting with others. Performing a self-talk prior to interacting is essential and can spare a lot of conflicts in the end. If you find that there are some hiccups in your conversation and you do not like the outcome take some time to stop, recall, and reflect on what just happened. Try your best to de-escalate the issue.

It is important to know that we each play a part in the communication breakdown. This is why it is essential to convey, what you believe you heard to obtain clarity on all sides. In serious cases, it is essential to follow up verbal communication in writing to assure that the discussion has been memorialized. This will help eliminate misunderstandings and allow you to make any corrections necessary.

If your messages are continually being misunderstood, you should begin to reflect on yourself, beginning with your past and how you were taught to communicate.

During various types of conversations some people feel rejected, feared or intimidated. We all have a voice, a story to tell, and a message to convey.

Healthy Relationships Are Important For Healing

If you can't feed a hundred people, then feed just one.

~Mother Teresa

People tend to focus on impacting large numbers and begin to give up if they can't influence many at one time. Any great leader knows that it takes only one beginning with self to make a difference and influence change. As a leader the focus should be on creating relationships. In order to create relationships, you must focus on the persons involved and how you will meet their needs. Meeting their needs can range from acknowledgment and appreciation to empowering creativity and independence.

According to the *Merriam-Webster Dictionary,* "Relationships represent the state of affairs existing between those having relations or dealings." Relationships develop in so many ways and places, from the grocery store and workplace to the medical industry. Healthy relationships are important because they can influence healing.

Let's look at how frequencies—from toxic to healthy—can tremendously impact the outcome in our everyday lives. Below are some illustrations inspired by a true story to help you better understand how this process works. The names and illnesses have been changed to protect their privacy.

ILLUSTRATION #1

Dr. Watson: "Ms. Hendricks, congratulations on your retirement. I'm sorry to hear that you're sick. Judging by your symptoms, you may have (illness). Let's do some tests to confirm this diagnosis and then begin working on some medications and treatments to help you live with this illness and possibly prolong your life."

In this illustration the idea of what the illness could be was quickly diagnosed, possibly based on the doctor's medical knowledge, or by his truth before any tests were taken. Ms. Hendricks was already experiencing a host of toxic frequencies within herself prior to going to the doctor due to her own internal fears and that of her family members that frequently reminded her of what generational diseases and illnesses that had plagued the family. Once she heard this diagnosis she immediately reacted to the doctor by believing what she heard.

All of these frequencies fed off of each other and created a final result. Clearly, you've seen this type of behavior in different scenarios that have been played out in your life. When toxic frequencies from either party collectively transmit low frequencies in order to color correct, you must stop riding on the low spectrum and self-work must begin.

Always remember before communicating with another person that everyone carries within themselves multiple layers that include some level of toxic frequencies. The difference is that, while some people continually work through these filters and layers to improve how they communicate, others will do little correction and accept their behavior, believing that attempting to be a good person is enough to correct any form of miscommunication.

Do not be frustrated or take it personally if you encounter those who refuse to do their self-work to improve their tainted or toxic color frequencies. At times, people are clearly aware that their behaviors can wreak havoc, not only with themselves but with those they encounter. The goal is to always be mindful of your self-talk, and approach any conversation with careful consideration when interacting and trying to connect with someone new or different. You can only change one person, yourself.

In order to clearly demonstrate the essence of having a healthy relationship, let's go back to the story about Ms. Hendricks. Ms. Hendricks was already experiencing a host of toxic frequencies within herself before going to the doctor. She believed the doctor spoke the truth because of what she was already feeling about herself causing her to feel that her life was over.

If she had felt and believed differently about herself, the outcome of her thoughts and what she heard and felt about the message would have been received differently. When two or more skewed world views impact each other, it influences the conversation as well as the outcome. Let's explore the conversation between Ms. Hendricks and the doctor, of what actually happened:

ILLUSTRATION #2

Dr. Watson: "Ms. Hendricks, how are you feeling today? How's the family? Congratulations on your retirement. I'm sorry to hear that you're sick. Based upon your symptoms, it can be any number of things, so let's do some tests to further gauge what's happening."

"After the tests, I'll be better able to determine what our next steps will be. It's my goal as your doctor to assure that you're at your optimal health and that you can finish enjoying your new life after retirement. We'll be working together on whatever the diagnosis is within the next few weeks."

Ms. Hendricks stated that, after the lab tests and blood work, she and her doctor had a discussion about the results. He then prescribed some medication for her illness, but she indicated that due to her internal toxic frequencies that had been kicking in, she had become confused and fearful during their conversation and everything that he said to her went over her head. Since there had been a personable, trusting patient-doctor relationship over the years, she thoroughly respected the doctor's opinion and chose not to ask too many questions and decided to just go home so that she could process what just happened.

It wasn't until about six months later, at her follow-up appointment, that things changed. She had been feeling better about herself and had been improving her self-talk because she wanted to remain healthy. When her regular doctor was unavailable, she had to see another doctor. As the other doctor began going over Ms. Hendricks' test results from six months ago, there were some words that totally shocked Ms. Hendricks. The doctor stated, "It appears that your (illness) is in remission."

Ms. Hendricks was shocked and asked, "What illness?" When she asked this doctor what it all meant, she learned that she had an illness that could have been detrimental if it had not been caught in time. Ms. Hendricks further stated that if she had fully under-stood what Dr. Watson had tried to tell her six months ago, she probably would have been dead by now.

She believed that if she had not trusted him, and had totally understood what he had been trying to tell her, that it could have taken her into a downward mental spiral. And knowing that she had an illness of that type would have been enough to kill her as well. As you can see from this example, there are so many variations of how high, low, and toxic frequencies can affect and influence the outcome of any type of conversation and situation.

How you set the stage in your mind and heart determines whether it festers into a conflict or develops into high (positive) results. As shown in the Illustrations it was her perception and trust that caused the outcome by how she interpreted it. She felt she could trust Dr. Watson; they had a personable relationship which caused her to focus less on her own self talk (which generated low frequencies) during their initial meeting.

She further stated that even if Dr. Watson was exhibiting some low frequencies she (due to their history) would have chosen to ignore it and instead focus on why she was there in the first place. Upon further discussion she realized that the only person that she could control was herself and her response. This example further illustrates how our minds and mental state can be impacted, which in turn influences us in many ways. Healthy relationships are essential for healing.

In all forms of communication, you must keep the goal clear and at the forefront (remaining within your high frequency) despite whatever obstacles that may occur— and they will. Every day you must make a conscious effort on how you will transmit your frequencies. What we think or speak can become our reality, so we must be careful because it can influence our lives.

Our self-talk and how we interpret information changes the message outcome. This is why it's important for the medical, education and law enforcement professionals to monitor their communication frequencies with groups or individuals when interacting. It also impacts the deescalation, healing and quick recovery process after dealing with any issue mentally, physically and spiritually. The outcomes of these frequency interactions misinterpretation or perception can greatly impact and influence life or death.

Healing Takes Time

Healing is a matter of time, but it is sometimes also a matter of opportunity.

~Hippocrates

We all must understand that it takes time to heal. In healing, a platform is created that provides an opportunity to get better by correcting the hurt. Let's explore some simple yet essential steps to healing that will assist you in the COLOR CORRECTION process:

~: Set your focus on becoming the results you seek. Any messages you receive must be positively transmitted from within. How you receive the message and respond to it is vital.

~: Imagine and reflect on the sole desire of what you are seeking. Begin to fully embody the results that you desire within your Spirit.

~: Continually focus your communication efforts within the high spectrum of your color frequency.

~: *Fuhgeddaboudit.* Forget about it, don't worry about it. Acknowledge what you feel but don't marry it. Work through your feelings, even the most difficult parts. When times get tough and challenges occur, your initial reaction should be to concentrate on the transmission of high color frequency messages.

~: Assess yourself more closely by listening to what you are telling yourself. Then begin to concentrate on what you are saying when you are talking to others.

~: Are you listening to what the person is saying or is your perception clouding you from receiving the message?

~: Are you obtaining the results you desire?

Whenever you communicate, the objective is to think "balance." Concentrate on balance. Find common ways to begin to consciously listen to the color frequency of others.

Even if you do not like what is being conveyed by the other party, or you believe their communication frequency is blatantly low, you must continue to hold the power to neutralize the situation or circumstance and positively change the frequency of the environment. Never judge others by your own story, by who you think they are or represent, just as you, they have their own unique story to tell. There is knowledge and a tremendous exchange of information within diverse circles.

Diversity brings change, new ideas, and creative ways of getting things done, just like we saw in the inventor and investor example. This is why several inventions like Tesla, Apple Watch, Uber, and various types of Social Media platforms exist today due to the uniqueness that was heard, accepted and embraced.

Acknowledging who you really are can be difficult to face. At first it may feel strange but you must begin to accept the color frequencies of others, especially those you do not understand or who look, act, or speak differently. You will be amazed to discover what you are missing if you allow others to be themselves.

It only takes one to make a change, one to be changed, and one to make a difference.

~Vernita Naylor

It is always important to remember that since you are working through your COLOR CORRECTION process, on a regular basis, that some people may not want to change or work on themselves. Let others grow and experience their COLOR CORRECTION journey at their own pace. The only behavior that you can control is yours so lead by example in how you talk, transmit, react and respond to others.

Acceptance of others is what marks the key to success. Let others know they are important and that they matter. People must be given a chance to express themselves in their own unique way. You may not understand initially but you must give them a chance to be heard.

Understand that anything worth doing takes times. Be patient, healing is a process and things will get better. Look for the change. You will notice that the negativity that once arose when faced with a challenge is no longer normal to you and now uncomfortable. Welcome the new you.

Don't pretend. Don't avoid. Don't be subjective. Focus more on maintaining balance, less on controlling and developing an understanding with all parties involved, while creating a safe place for being heard.

Become A Leader—Others Will Follow

There is no foot so small that it cannot leave an imprint on this world.

~Anonymous

If you lead, and do so effectively, others will follow. Always executing proper communication is key while diligently working to successfully connect. If the persons that you are trying to interact with chooses to operate with toxic frequencies don't stoop to their level, recognize the behavior but see how you can lead by example.

Working through your journey of forgiveness and no longer living in the past is one of the components that makes a leader. This is especially crucial for those who have witnessed you during your early journey and now see you doing the work. Your victory encourages others; they began to believe that they too are capable of such change.

Leaders lead and know when to follow. Leaders set an example and do not get caught up in what others are doing. Leaders are proactive and do not wait for others to set the stage. Leaders look for solutions especially in the most difficult circumstances or environments.

When you lead in a healthy space things work, projects get done, others become more proactive and motivated leaving more people happy and fulfilled. As a leader you may not know what's inside of others but as a good leader you will notice and acknowledge change within them that is positive.

Being comfortable with yourself, and knowing your color frequency while being transparent and allowing others to see your progress connects you to others. People are always watching. What do they see when they look at you? Do they see someone that they can trust? Do they feel encouraged?

When people see positive changes in others it can either influence or discourage them depending upon where they are in their own journey. During times of crisis you really get to see what people are made of and who they really are. You can be greatly influenced due to what you see, hear, or read through external communication, including social media, radio, print or TV. Most times, biases (or Isms) behavior seems to appear to be familiar or normal to individuals in a subtle way.

EXAMPLE

~: *You are at the grocery store and someone 6'2" and approximately 250 lbs walks towards you and you find yourself clutching your purse or wallet and begin to feel threatened. WHY? Could it be that they are more scared of you than you are of them?*

~: *You find a group of same sex individuals at the park laughing, joking, touching and enjoying themselves. You are uncomfortable. WHY? Could it be that they are old classmates and haven't seen each other in years?*

~: *You must converse with a group that seems to be of mature age based on their grey hair. You feel that you will not be understood and will face continuous conflict. WHY? Could it be that these individuals are closer to your age than you think and may hold the same views or outlook as you?*

~: *You discover a group of individuals sitting in front of your neighbor's house. You noticed that some of them are wearing cornrows, and have tattoos wearing urban clothing. As time goes on you begin to consider whether you should contact law enforcements. WHY? Could it be that they are gathered at the home of a family friend and visiting from medical, law and/or business school?*

As in these example it is your perception of the narrative that you see and have learned from your experiences which is causing you to feel threatened, intimidated or judging incorrectly. Despite our differences it is the diversity that creates uniqueness and provide solutions in communicating to the path for obtaining positive results. Never assume that you know a person's story at first glance. If you decide to delve deeper you will discover that there are more similarities than differences.

Correcting Broken Communication Patterns

I imagine one of the reasons people cling to their hates so stubbornly is because they sense, once hate is gone, they will be forced to deal with pain.

~James Baldwin

It is difficult to think freely when you feel trapped or broken. Bias or Isms can be challenging to overcome this is why some people remain as they are well into adulthood although they see that it's destroying their lives and those around them. When we encounter others, an explosion happens that sometimes creates something wonderful, while at others times the outcome can be disastrous.

Most times disaster occurs because we do not trust what we do not understand. At this stage, people can cause a wedge, create obstacles, or hinder the outcome of anything that they are involved in. They have allowed their bias and unhealed emotions to take center stage. Trust is essential in order to incorporate and effectively use the COLOR CORRECTION process for communicating.

As Stephen M.R. Covey states in his book, *The Speed of Trust*, is that when trust is present things speed up.

What this means is that if there is trust amongst individuals, or groups, communication improves and the desired results can be achieved even in a toxic environment. It is important to understand that this process can take quite a while, but it can be done and things can be accomplished more effectively over time.

It is always essential that you communicate in such a way that everyone understands the message. If the message is not understood, there can be such disarray that nothing gets done. When the message is distorted or misunderstood this means that a breakdown in communication has occurred.

The breakdown quickly occurs when we begin to judge others based upon skin color, upbringing, culture, generation, religion, or other biases (or Isms). It is these Isms that must be changed through the COLOR CORRECTION process. To continue the COLOR CORRECTION process we must begin to change our thoughts, which begin to change the outcome.

By mastering the art of communicating, exercising your truth, and correcting how you communicate, your future gets brighter and better. Take small steps in how you improve your communication with others. A form of color correcting is to check in and begin working from the inside out, stop judging what you are looking at and perceiving from your narrow perspective.

Be open, and consider the possibilities. When introduced to anything new create a paradigm shift to acceptance, love, inclusion and forgiveness. Forgive yourself and forgive others of biases or Isms.

By taking these steps you are well on your way to begin the change you need to see in this world. With intentional practice, you will discover that with time and effort you can help create a more cohesive environment for all involved.

Put On Your Mask First

The eye sees only what the mind is prepared to comprehend.

~Henri-Louis Bergson

When you fly, the stewardess tells you the process and procedures of what to do in case of a change in cabin pressure. "In case of a loss of cabin pressure, the oxygen mask above your seat will deploy. Please place the mask first over your mouth and then assist your child or other passengers."

If you can't help yourself, how can you be an asset to others? Learn to be honest about all of your *own* toxic filter frequencies before you focus on the toxic frequencies of others. A good rule of thumb is to understand your triggers so that you can work on healing or minimizing the impact of them.

Knowing and embracing who we are, including our diversity and uniqueness is important. True, our experiences—even the bad ones—have shaped our reality, but once we understand why we are feeling the way we are, we must learn how to release the past and exude confidence in making the connection better for the future.

Only once we release, can we unleash negative emotions, exchange information and demonstrate how powerful and instrumental our frequencies can be collectively despite the differences. In the world, we can't do anything alone; we must rely on and work with each other.

In the process of correcting, it is important to face what is wrong and not avoid those parts of who we are, pretend they are not there or that we are not bothered by them. As others begin to see how genuine you are and your consistency in communicating, they too will begin to embrace this and challenge themselves to be better. On occasion you may get asked several questions about your process and the challenges that you faced while making this paradigm shift including some of your fears.

Embrace this moment to speak truth and transparency. As you begin to transition into your pattern of healing another aspect of the color correcting process is the element of mindfulness. Mindfulness is a combination of love, kindness, and awareness.

Mindfulness is essential because it resonates with a high vibration of the positive spectrum and improves your health to begin a new, unrestricted life for yourself and others. You only have one life to live, and how you live it is up to you. Each of us live separate lives; don't stay trapped in the abyss of biases, Isms or unforgiveness. Begin to take the step necessary for your healing now!

Focus on the fact that when dealing with people or situations your purpose is to positively influence all that you encounter. By doing this, the universe pays you back for the positive karma you have transmitted to others. What you are giving is not only positive influence; you are returning the gift that was given to you by the Creator. This gift is not for you to hold on to; it is for you to give and to be shared with others.

Life is about karma and reciprocity, so be mindful of what you expel or transmit to others, because it will come back to you, both the good and bad. As you positively empty yourself, you allow the universe to give unto you. In creating these channels, it is absolutely necessary to consider that each generation brings with it something different and that life is a continual ebb and flow.

You will discover that people tend to be more intimidated by who they think we are and less by whom we actually are.

~Vernita Naylor

As you begin to connect with others and open up, you will learn more about them, their story and their truth. Continually operating within the COLOR CORRECTION process, you begin to change, improve and operate within a continual flow of a high frequency. This process is never done and is an important part of learning and growth.

Focus on your communication and the rest will take care of itself.

COLOR CORRECTION ASSESSMENT: IMPROVE YOUR NARRATIVE

"I remained too much inside my head and ended up losing my mind."

~Edgar Allan Poe

Improve the Narrative of Your Conversations

People do not realize that there are a lot of tragedies that begin in the mind. Some people get so locked up inside their heads that they create stories that are unreal. The irony is that they believe the stories so much that it becomes their reality.

To better understand something or someone the goal is to research. How you research is to ask and seek for answers, the correct answers, not the answers that you choose to believe is true.

When you find yourself operating within the low spectrum—especially around others—try excusing yourself by going outside, to a restroom stall, or into the hall, where you can discreetly give yourself a break and regroup.

Regroup by taking a deep breath, thinking of something positive, and reciting several affirmations to calm and redirect your energy. Continue this process for about five to seven minutes until you truly feel in sync with your high-emotional frequencies. If you don't have an affirmation that you can connect with at the moment, here are a few affirmations you can consider using and repeat as needed:

- ~: I am in control of my emotions.
- ~: I am in control of my reactions.
- ~: I will not let the toxic frequencies within me hold me hostage.
- ~: I will not let the toxic frequencies of others bind me.
- ~: I am love. I am peace. I am free. I am no longer bound.
- ~: I am _____. (Fill in the blank.)
- ~: I am _____. (Fill in the blank.)
- ~: I am _____. (Fill in the blank.)

If you believe you need more time beyond the five to seven minutes, take it. If you are in a leadership capacity and not operating effectively as a leader, it will not be productive if you shortchange yourself and others by proceeding with the task at hand when you are not at your best. Continue this process, even when you go back into the meeting, to avoid operating within the toxic frequencies that could be operating within the environment or room.

You must understand that high and low frequencies are simultaneously operating around us at all times, and you must be prepared. There are times that you should exercise COLOR CORRECTION not only before but during and after a meeting when interacting with individuals or groups. As reflected in the assessment test there are both low and high influences to everyone's behavior, character or personality traits just like astrology or the personality tests. Remain positive especially during challenging times.

Continue to document and assess whether you are growing or declining in your communication. This process takes time because it reflects a new way of thinking, listening, hearing, and processing. If you begin to experience a trigger due to a toxic frequency, regardless of whether it arrived from something within or an outside source, harness your focus back to your middle spectrum and work towards your positive spectrum.

Consider using your journal and analysis charts to help you do this. Remember, your goal is to always assure that those you are trying to connect with feel safe and have their voices heard. When they feel safe and their voices are being heard, people will feel they are being included, and they will contribute openly and freely toward the collective goal.

These principles are what create a more cohesive conversation that garners the results you desire. Remember, diversity represents unique ideas, creative exchanges of information, and out-of-the-box, unconventional thinking.

Never give up.

Now That We
Have Your Attention

Again, we thank you for purchasing this book and becoming a part of the *Speaking In Colors* Movement. In this book you have been given an understanding of the four concepts of the color frequency process—THE FREQUENCY you were BORN WITH, THE FREQUENCY given by NATURE VS. NURTURE, TRANSMITTING FREQUENCY and COLOR CORRECTION FREQUENCY—as they relate to speaking and connecting whether you are operating within multiple generational environments or working with various people encountering biases or Isms.

We use the *Speaking in Colors* concept in our personal and professional lives and have discovered that it actually works. Just as we have been able to do, you too are now more equipped to move forward in communicating your true frequency intent and getting the results that you desire. After evaluating what your color frequency is and how it is that you communicate, you will now learn and understand how to neutralize your low frequencies and the way you perceive information while creating a path for connecting.

With change in how you communicate, you can affect not only one but many one step at a time. Using this process and the tools will provide you with a clearer way to connect and communicate while minimizing the toxic frequencies that are often transmitted during conversations. It is important to understand that COLOR CORRECTION is always a work in progress.

You will discover that you have to tweak and continue to neutralize some of the toxic frequencies that may cloud how your frequency speaks to others but keep working at it. Color correcting is never done, or perfected but merely improved. As you continue to journal and analyze your charts you will begin to see a lot of improvement.

It is not your job to correct others; it *is* your job to correct yourself. Be in control of how you react, respond, and connect with what is being said, whether you agree with it or not. If you continue to use the *Speaking in Colors* concept, it will be felt by others, it will allow room for others to do the same, and growth will occur. This does not mean that you will always agree with the message being conveyed, but you will be able to neutralize yourself and the conversations enough to respectfully agree to disagree.

Agreeing to disagree will allow you the ability to leave your own values intact as you exhibit a reciprocal honor and respect for the opinion and views of others. Our hope is that this book gives you an understanding and a glimpse into how this concept can help you in obtaining the results and reach the goals you seek. In creating a safe space where we can all coexist and not worry about being judged, we can help to remove judgment and live together more cohesively.

Speaking in Colors **is not only a concept, it's** *A MOVEMENT!*

JOIN THE MOVEMENT

Welcome to the Speaking in Colors Community. We want to hear from you. Connect with us! https://jabezenterprisegroup.com/speakingincolors/

ABOUT THE AUTHORS

Vernita Naylor

Mother, Educator, Small Business Advocate,
Change Agent, Cultural Equity Advisor, Speaker,
Business Owner, Published Author

Vernita Naylor is a California Bay Area native. For over 30 years she has been educating, advocating and supporting diverse business owners in various industry platforms from music and entertainment and supply chain management to government contracting. She works heavily within the Diversity, Equity and Inclusion (DEI) industry as a Cultural Equity Advisor and penned the book, Get the Cheese, Avoid the Traps: An Interactive Guide to Government Contracting, to help improve the economic marketplace and enhance the supplier diversity and government contracting program in partnership with small business owners, buying agencies and building capacity partners ranging from Small Business Development Centers (SBDC) and Procurement Technical Assistance Centers (PTAC) to Chambers of Commerce. Her passion is to prepare diverse businesses to become business, contract and supplier ready for viability to work in the supplier diversity and government contracting industry in partnership with government and corporate buying agencies.

Vernita is so excited to work with her daughter, Nikita Nikol; an exceptional trailblazing young lady who is an Entrepreneur, making strides in the world, by bringing *Speaking in Colors* to you. Her vision is that people experience the success that they seek in how they communicate with each other regardless of their industry.

Nikita Nikol Naylor

Daughter, Entrepreneur, Healing & Holistic Advocate,
Beauty Professional, Spiritual Illuminist

Nikita Nikol is a California Bay Area native. She has always been inclined to understanding with empathy. Having a strong desire to beautify the world, she began her career in the beauty industry at a very young age. During this time, she learned the true importance of clear communication, public relations, and customer service. She is a lover of words and believes communication—both verbal and nonverbal—is the key source to knowledge, understanding, and acceptance. Being a successful business owner with over 18 years in the beauty and public relations industries has inspired her to partner with her mother, Vernita, to bring you *Speaking in Colors*.

www.ingramcontent.com/pod-product-compliance
Lightning Source LLC
Chambersburg PA
CBHW050731030426
42336CB00012B/1505